HISTORY CONCOURSE 2005

A Celebration
of the Life and Work of
Professor Ebiegberi Joe Alagoa

Edited by

Nkparom C. Ejituwu
Abi A. Derefaka
Atei M. Okorobia
David A. Alagoa
John H. Enemugwem

Onyoma Research Publications

© 2005 Onyoma Research and The Contributors

ISBN: 978-37314-3-2

Published in 2005 by
Onyoma Research Publications
11 Orogbum Crescent, GRA Phase II
P.O. Box 8611, Federal Secretariat Post Office
Port Harcourt, Rivers State, Nigeria

E-mail: kala_joe@yahoo.com
Website: www.onyoma.org
Mobile: 0803-308-3385
0805-942-1883

Printed by
Doval Ventures Limited
12 Ohaeto Street, D/Line
Port Harcourt, Rivers State
08033075443

**Word Processing,
Type Selection and Layout:**
Jigekuma Ayebatari Ombu
at Hisis (Publishing) Ltd • Port Harcourt
0803 300 4589

CONTRIBUTORS

Adiele E. Afigbo, NNOM, FNAL, FHSN, Professor Emeritus, Ebonyi State University, Abakaliki

Ebiegberi Joe Alagoa, FNAL, FHSN, Professor Emeritus, University of Port Harcourt, Choba

Bolanle Awe, FNAL, Professor of History, University of Ibadan, Ibadan; Pro-Chancellor, University of Nigeria, Nsukka

Winston I. Bell-Gam, Professor of Geography and Environmental Management, Dean, School of Graduate Studies, University of Port Harcourt, Choba

Bobo Sofiri Brown, JP, President and Chairman, Governing Council, Nigeria Institute of Public Relations

Abi A. Derefaka, PhD, Senior Lecturer, History and Archaeology, University of Port Harcourt, Choba

Nkparom C. Ejituwu, Professor of History, University of Port Harcourt, Choba

John H, Enemugwem, PhD, Senior Lecturer, History, University of Port Harcourt, Choba

Tam Fiofori, Journalist, Photographer, Film Maker

Alabo Dagogo M.J. Fubara, Professor of Geodesy, Rivers State University of Science and Technology, Port Harcourt

Robin Horton, Professor of Anthropology and Religion; Sir James Fraser Lecturer, University of Cambridge, Cambridge, UK; Corresponding Member of the British Academy; Amanyanabo of Kalabari Merit Award for Academic Contributions

Mamerhi J. Igben, Principal Librarian, Rivers State University of Science and Technology, Port Harcourt

Alabo S.O. Sunday Jaja, PhD, Senior Lecturer in History, University of Calabar, Calabar

Atei Mark Okorobia, PhD, Senior Lecturer in History, University of Port Harcourt, Choba

Jigekuma A. Ombu, Publisher at Hisis (Publishing) Ltd, Port Harcourt

Kingdom Eke Orji, PhD, Chief Lecturer, Rivers State College of Arts and Science, Port Harcourt

Sereba Agiobu-Kemmer Pearse, Cultural Consultant

S.I. Udoidem, Professor of Philosophy; Dean, Faculty of Humanities, University of Port Harcourt, Choba

Okon E. Uya (Ambassador), FNAL, FHSN, Professor of History, University of Calabar, Calabar

CONTENTS

Contributors			iii
Plates			vii
1	Introduction	Nkparom N.C. Ejituwu	1
2	Alagoa: The Philosopher	S.I. Udoidem	5
3	Alagoa: Oral Tradition and the Multi-Method Approach	Robin Horton	29
4	Alagoa as Pioneer of Oral Tradition and Oral History in the Niger Delta	Nkparom C. Ejituwu and J.H. Enemugwem	43
5	Keeping the Faith	E.J. Alagoa	51
6	The Torch is Passed Over: Response to Keeping the Faith	Okon E. Uya	57
7	Professor E.J. Alagoa: A Cultural Nationalist	Bolanle Awe	67
8	Professor E.J. Alagoa: The Administrator	Abi A. Derefaka	79
9	The X-Factor in the Life and Work of Professor E.J. Alagoa	Sereba Agiobu-Kemmer Pearse	91
10	Alagoa as an Intellectual Leader	Atei Mark Okrobia and Kingdom Eke Orji	111
11	The Essence of E.J. Alagoa	Adiele E. Afigbo	127
Supplement: History Meets Jaja of Opobo			131
1	Address Presented to King Dandeson Jaja	Abi A. Derefaka	133

2	'History Meets Jaja of Opobo': Introductory Remarks on the Concourse	Tam Fiofori	137
3	Address of Welcome	HRM King Dandeson Jaja	139
4	Past and Present: History of Development in Opobo	S.O. Jaja	143
5	Environmental Issues of Concern in 'Opobo Kingdom	Dagogo M.J. Fubara	149
6	Towards the Sustainable Development of Opobo Kingdom	Winston I. Bell-Gam	165
7	A New Local Economy to Re-Invent Opobo Kingdom: Notes on a Development Model for the Niger Delta and Other Zones of Nigeria	Bobo Sofiri Brown	171

History Concourse 2005: Attendance Register		179
Chapter References and Select Bibliography	Jigekuma A. Ombu	183
Index	Mamerhi J. Igben	197

Plate 1: Participants at the *Concourse*

Plate 2: *Concourse* Members with HRM King Dandeson Jaja, Amanyanabo of Opobo and his Council of Chiefs

1

Introduction

Nkparom C. Ejituwu

This collection of papers emerged from the gathering of the cream of the historical profession at Professor Alagoa's residence in Port Harcourt on 30th April 2005. Tagged **History Concourse 2005**, it consisted of a small group of close friends and associates of Professor E.J. Alagoa, friends such as Emeritus professor Adiele E. Afigbo and Ambassador Okon E. Uya, Bolanle Awe and Abdullahi Mahadi, who gathered to celebrate the life and work of Professor E.J. Alagoa. Although he was supposed to have retired from the University of Port Harcourt at the age of seventy, he was actually carrying greater and heavier loads. He was, for instance, the Chairman of the **Ijaw History Project** with possibility of extensive field-work in the Niger Delta and the Diaspora. He was also Pro-Chancellor of the Niger Delta University at the Wilberforce Island, Bayelsa State as well as Chairman of Onyoma Research Publications. In all, therefore, the *Concourse* was an occasion for the celebration of academic excellence and dedication to duty.

The seminar that was part of the *Concourse* brought together papers from scholars. For instance, Bolanle Awe, presented a paper on "Alagoa: A Cultural Nationalist"; S.I. Udoidem, "Alagoa as an African Philosopher", and Nkparom C. Ejituwu and John H. Enemugwem, "Alagoa as Pioneer of Oral

Tradition and Oral History in the Niger Delta". Others are Abi A. Derefaka, "Alagoa as an Administrator"; Mrs Sereba Agiobu-Kemmer Pearse, "The X Factor in Professor E.J. Alagoa's Life and Work"; Atei Mark Okorobia, "Alagoa as a Community and Intellectual Leader; and E.J. Alagoa's "Keeping the Faith", responded to by Uya's "Response to Keeping the Faith".

Two of the papers or comments made during paper presentation were very revealing in terms of the role played by Professor Alagoa as an intellectual. These were Emeritus Professor Afigbo's observation that Alagoa may look "frail" but his intellectual output was such that it could move mountains. Professor Horton, on his part, said he and Alagoa were often seen as antagonists, but in reality, Alagoa was his source of strength and survival at the University of Port Harcourt. He (Professor Horton) was often seen as a radical but each time his radicalism landed him in trouble, it was Alagoa who bailed him out of it. So, where was their antagonism?

Some of the scholars did not present papers and they served as Lead Discussants. These included Professor Abdullahi Mahadi, Professor A.E. Afigbo and Dr Gabriel Okara, the poet and novelist. The totality of the presentations was a brilliant rendition of intellectual discourse at the *Concourse*.

Professor E.J. Alagoa is a lover of art work and so, the organisers of the *Concourse* brought some budding artists to exhibit their work in celebration of the life and work of Professor E.J. Alagoa. They were Pius Waritimi who specialized in the exhibition of the realities and the plight of the Niger Delta; Perrin Oglafa who specialized on signs and symbols with emphasis on the abstract; Palmore Abassah whose artistic orientation was expressionistic and consisted of interpretation of life with colour, texture, pattern and form. Also invited was Diseye Tantua, whose work was impressionistic; asking question of life through fine art Under the theme of "Colours, Myths and Realities from Bayelsa", they exhibited their art-work and specialities from 30th April - 7th May, 2005. The TSSK Theatre Company and Dr H.L. Bell-Gam also provided an evening of entertainment.

It is difficult to mention all these people without providing a space for the "X Factor in Professor E.J. Alagoa's Life and Work", namely, Lady Mercy G. Alagoa.

The programme was completed with a visit to Opobo where Professor Alagoa and his colleagues were received by the **Amanyanabo** of Opobo, HRM King Dandeson Jaja at his palace. It was a wonderful occasion.

2

Alagoa: The Philosopher

S. Iniobong Udoidem

A fundamental question that this paper intends to resolve is whether a historian can be a philosopher. If the answer is in the affirmative, then our reflection on Ebiegberi Joe Alagoa as a philosopher is justifiable. In order to instantiate our case, this paper would seek to examine the person and works of Ebiegberi Joe Alagoa the historian from a philosophical perspective. The method we will adopt is an approach by which Alagoa through the various texts speaks for himself. By this I mean that we will quote passages from his works and then do some analysis to bring out their philosophical import.

Who is a Philosopher?

In its ordinariness, a philosopher is one who searches for knowledge by taking note of, and paying attention to the little things around his universe of existence, thinks about them, speculates about them, uses them as the stepping stone for interpreting and understanding the more profound and distant objects of consciousness.

According to Aristotle's philosophical pragmatics, everybody who desires or seeks knowledge is a philosopher. But by the Socratic aporetic method, it takes only the Philosopher to know how and why all seekers of knowledge are philosophers. The thesis of the essay is that a philosopher, whether considered in its ordinariness or in its philosophical sophistication could be found in the person and works of Professor E.J. Alagoa.

Professor E.J. Alagoa, a son of Nembe in Bayelsa State, in Nigeria, Africa. His search for knowledge began from Nembe. He learned the culture of the Nembe, thought about it and used the Nembe culture to reach the Niger Delta, used the Niger Delta to reach Nigeria and from Nigeria to Africa and the world. From the pedestal of a higher learning he returns to Nembe and the Niger Delta with a new understanding and appreciation of what is indigenous to the Niger Delta not as something new but as that which he had always known. Alagoa began his search for knowledge with oral history among the Niger Delta with the discovery that all histories are oral and that only when reflected uopn, interpreted and documented do they become scientific in the popular sense (I call it science in the popular sense because orality has its own logic and science). After his years of studies he returned to the Niger Delta to redeem its history in its orality.

A philosopher, who searches for knowledge questions, speculates, interprets and then narrates and probably documents his findings can be seen as a historian of some sort while a historian who interprets events and objects of experience could be said to be a philosopher. In this sense both the philosopher and the historian are interpreters of human objects of consciousness. Probably, it is in this context that Alagoa defines history as "the study of man through the evidence of his past actions."[1] Having situated Alagoa the historian as a possible philosopher, our task would be to examine his works with the hope of highlighting elements that are uniquely philosophical in terms of their fundamentality.

E.J. On the Philosophy of History: Hindsight as Foresight

In the Preface to the book, *The Uses of Hindsight as Foresight*, Alagoa enunciates what might be regarded as his philosophy of history. He begins with the following questions:

> Do historians teach, reflect or simply tell stories to delight their listeners or readers? For the present, these offerings merely represent a record of what one historian believed and recounted to some audience. In this sense, they may tell us as much about the historian as the historian wishes to tell about the world about him.[2]

To the question of whether the historian who historicizes engages in a reflective activity or whether his story-telling actually teaches, one could easily respond affirmatively. That yes, history is a reflective activity and the historian who engages in narration of his experience is actually teaching. But Alagoa raised a more philosophical issue about historical activity, namely that it is a record of what one historian believed (or believes) and recounted (recounts) to some audience. Alagoa captures these ideas when he notes that his story about the Niger Delta is the story of the Niger Delta about itself and intended for the Niger Deltans. He wrote: "The talks to public audiences attempt to turn whatever insights may have been gained from academic study of the deep past into public enlightenment about the present and the recent past."[3]

Here Alagoa affirms that historization is subjective activity and that its mode of narration and the content of what is narrated are always targeted on an audience. The narration, being his own **story (history)** is actually a story about the world around him, his story is only a tiny piece of the big whole which he is not able to see. He therefore admits that his work as a historian is only to tell part of the story in an imperfect way. Alagoa admits:

> We must accept the story of the blind men feeling parts of an elephant and making individual efforts to define an elephant as instructive. We can only tell part of the story in imperfect terms.[4]

The only question that one might raise here without wanting to attempt an answer is: if history is so subjective and limited in its immediate universe of experience, is there any possibility of objective and universal claims? Alagoa adopts two approaches in responding to this question. The first one is a pragmatic approach and the second is a philosophical approach.

In the pragmatic approach, Alagoa recalls how the history of the slave trade, the palm oil trade and the striking of mineral oil in the Niger Delta affected and changed the history of the Nigerian nation into world market consciousness. Alagoa noted:

The region has been part of the international slave trade from the fifteenth century through the seventeenth century when it was a significant portion of what was termed the Slave Coast of West Africa. From the late eighteenth through the nineteenth century it came to be better known as the Oil Rivers, supplying a great deal of the palm oil and kernel required by Britain to maintain its leadership position in the industrial revolution. In the twentieth and twenty first century, the region has become the centre of Nigerian crude oil supply exploited by several international oil companies.[5]

Here we have a practical example of how the private histories of the Niger Delta people have impacted the whole world, thus confirming Alagoa's claim that a private community history has universal implications.

The philosophical approach to the resolution of the problem of the particularity of history (or subjectivity) and its objectivity is to be found in what Alagoa describes as the dialectics of history. It should be noted here that what Alagoa means by dialectics is not to be understood in the Hegelian or Marxian sense but in the inculturational sense[6] wherein the present is the given culture through which the historian reflects on the past, and the past is brought to the present not as present but as the past remembered in the light of the present. This new past is not the past as it was but as past remembered in the light of new realities or, to put it differently, as past remembered by the present. The thing that should be noted here is that it not everything of the past that is remembered but only that which the present considers relevant and purposeful. This means that the present is a constitutive determinant of the past and in how and what is remembered. This new past is projected into the future as the basis for prediction. It was on the basis of this interculturational approach that Alagoa developed his philosophy of history rendering **Hindsight as Foresight.**

HIND (SIGHT) ⇌ SIGHT ⇌ FORE (SIGHT)

PAST ⇌ PRESENT ⇌ FUTURE

From the pictogram above we see that **sight** is present both in the **hind** and in the **fore**. It is evident that the **sight** (present) through memory selectively brings from the hind (past) only that which is relevant to the present on the basis of which **fore** (future) is projected. The implication is that in this philosophy of history we see some element of humanism and an existentialist construct. The active involvement of the present in the determination of what is remembered of the past and in what is projected of the future makes the "existential now" or what Alagoa calls the "time present" very humanistic. In his discussion on the notion of time and development he employs African proverbs to reinforce his interpretation of history. According to him time present falls between time future and time past. He demonstrates this in the following Nembe proverbs:

Irusi / Igoin di (Laziness breeds poverty).[7]

As explained by Alagoa, this present draws from the past, as its moral validity lies in experience. Yet the maxim itself is intended for application in the present, to save people from falling into destitution in the future.

Dorigha kana / fun tangha (An unwoven basket cannot carry dirt).[8]

In the interpretation of this proverb, Alagoa says that this is a present oriented truism derived from past experience, used to persuade to action in the present to provide for the future.[9] Another African proverb from the Ikwerre Alagoa employs to support his philosophy states thus:

Dikne churo be bisi anwa evulu n'anwu / obita atnur joomu yanu a evulu nga o zi budnu (A man who wants a ram to be slaughtered at his grave side, should keep an ewe to produce the ram while he is alive).[10]

In his explanation he says:

> We are dealing with a time capable of treatment through foresighted action in which we prepare ourselves for the future time. planning in advance so that at the appropriate future date, our expectations may be fulfilled. Here human expectations are clearly linked to experience of past events that recur, so that our expectations of their recurring in the future are realistic. In the case of death and attendant funeral envisaged, the future is in effect already known, and can be confidently planned for in the present.[11]

With this dialectics of history - the historization of the present (sight), he employs it to reflect on the history of the Ijaw and the Niger Delta. What he remembers about the past is conditioned by the present history of the Niger Delta, namely most wealthy, most exploited, most restive, etc. as noted by Alagoa:

> The Ijaw and the Niger Delta have been a significant part of the Nigerian region and are not amenable to silence, because of their significant contributions from antiquity to modern times. The Niger Delta has been a major centre of exchange of slaves and palm oil with the western world, and the people have been the middlemen between the Nigerian world and Atlantic Europe and America. At present it is the centre of the petroleum and gas industries of Nigeria, supplying upwards of 80% of the revenue of the Nigerian nation. Indeed, petroleum and gas have become such a crucial element of the Nigerian economy and so completely identified with the Niger Delta that the presence of these resources has become a defining criterion of what constitutes "Niger Delta".[12]

In another discourse Alagoa noted:

> The contemporary historian of Nigeria is confronted with issues arising from the condition of the Niger Delta, highlighted by

the conditions of abject poverty under which the Ijaw and other inhabitants of the region live. Nigeria is bound to deal with these issues to gain peace and a stable and secure environment in which to pursue its goals of economic and social development. The processes for the production of the petroleum and gas from the Niger Delta, and the political conditions put in place by the laws and constitution of Nigeria are not seen by the Ijaw and other peoples of the Niger Delta as fair and just. The objective material conditions in which the wealth of the Niger Delta is tapped and distributed determine the contemporary history of instability in the Niger Delta, and eventually, the history of the entire Federal Republic of Nigeria.[13]

Here Alagoa argues that the present condition of the Niger Delta is conditioned by the past and because the Niger Delta is so crucial to the economic and social development of Nigeria, the future of Nigeria does not only depend on the future of the Niger Delta but in correction of the historical injustices done to the people of the Niger Delta people.

Another interesting feature of Alagoa's philosophy of history is that it is futuristic. Having examined the history of the Niger Delta people he concludes poignantly that "for a people identified by a history of heroic struggle, there can only be hope in the future."[14] In another passage he noted, "a heritage of history is a storehouse of experience to be used to make progress in the present."[15]

What could be said from what has been examined so far of Alagoa's philosophy of history is that he is not only a theoretician but that he is also a pragmatist and a result oriented person. Because of the conviction and belief in hindsight as foresight he proposed that even a regrettable hindsight such as slavery can have a bright future. He has therefore championed the cause of the slave trade route tourism as an economic goldmine, a veritable means of human integration and a mediating structure for peace and reconciliation in the world.

One thing also that should be noted in our analysis of Alagoa's philosophy of history is that the only thing that is real is the present. Both the past and the future are as constructed by the present. The past is as distant as the future. As the past is close to the present, so is the possibility of accurate prediction of the future. But where the past is so distant and the fact unclear, so it is difficult to predict or manipulate the future. What is more, a past that is politicised makes the present unsuitable and the future bleak. Perhaps this is explanation of the Nigerian predicament. And for Alagoa it is because the history and the wealth of the Niger Delta have been so politically skewed, that is why the present is determinably unstable and the future unpredictable.

On what future can be predicted from the past and the present experiences, Alagoa has this to say:

> What future can we forecast for the people of the Niger Delta from our knowledge of their place in Nigerian history? Not a bright one if

we went solely by the present history of the failure of efforts to use democratic processes to effect change in the fortunes of the region. The present reveals only gloom. But the history of the Ijaw people, even as exemplified by the life of Adaka Boro, suggests that the future can yet bring hope for a people not given to despair. ...For a people identified by a history of heroic struggle, there can only be hope in the future. A people of courage like the lion, adaptable to land and water like the crocodile, can only strive for the stars.[16]

In this quotation we see a classic example of how Alagoa brings his philosophy of history to bear. It shows how the future (foresight), is predicated on the past (hindsight). The heroic past is presented as a hope for the future. It is important to note that it is only the heroic past and not the failure that is presented as the hope of the future.

Another interesting aspect of this philosophy of history is that there is an element of positivistic humanism. In the proverb that says that "a man who wants a ram to be slaughtered at his graveside, should keep an ewe to produce the ram while he is alive", while it is a warning one should prepare for the future, it does show that in the African context sometimes the future can be predicted and organized in such a way that what is to come is already guaranteed.

Alagoa on Time

One of the dimensions of Alagoa's thought that flows directly from his philosophy of history is his idea of time. If hindsight (which is a-has-been and is not anymore) can be construed as foresight (which is a-going-to be and is not yet), what is the distance between hindsight and foresight and how is it to be measured? The gap between the "has-been and is not anymore" and the other which "is-going-to-be and is not yet" is the "now" which "is". Yet the "now" which is, is always in a continuous flux, becoming past and becoming future. When there is a past, the future becomes the "now," and before one becomes conscious of it, the "now" becomes the past. The process continues *ad infinitum*. Yet the totality of these moments constitutes what is often referred to as "Time," whether it is historical time or past time or future time or passing time or eternal time. But, in this matrix, the time "now" cannot do without the "time past" and the time past cannot do without the "now." Similarly, the time "now" cannot do without the future and the future cannot do without the "now." In that internal dynamism of time the past cannot do without the future nor can the future do without the past.

In an attempt to come to terms with this complex reality Alagoa sought the benefit of hindsight by appealing to his African predecessor, the Berber philosopher from Tagaste in North Africa. There he discovered that Augustine's formulation of time was a case of African "concepts mediated by Western philosophical traditions"[17] especially the works of Plato and Aristotle. Yet, he found in Augustine something very indigenous and ingenious namely that Time is "nothing more than distention ... of mind."[18] To explain what Augustine meant, Alagoa said,

> The mind receives impressions of time in the present by intuition, but "passing time" known intuitively in the present also changes almost instantly into time past. The mind attempts to make sense of the impressions it receives of the process of constantly changing time: it considers the present, remembers the past, and looks forward to the future. As for the future, mind can only approach it through expectation and through prophecy.[19]

Alagoa explains further that for Augustine time moves from future (expectation) to the present (experienced through intuition), to the past (in memory) with the present occupying the centre stage.[20]

It should be noted that Augustine's position of perceiving the totality of time as one was African but in the attempt to give exact measure like in the Western science, he was forced to locate time in the future.[21] He was probably influenced by Plato's ideal types which exist in the supra sensible world where the human soul hopes to attain knowledge when it returns. It is this hope (expectation) of return from which Augustine's time takes its beginning. This Augustinian cosmology and its notion of time being rested on the future is made manifest in his text, *The City of God*. Here he distinguishes between the City of God and the City of Man.

The City of God is presented as the future glory after which the city of man must be modeled if the city of man (earth) is to be peaceful and habitable.

In his own contribution Alagoa notes that historical time which is his own concern as an historian focuses on the past. However, he discovers that even the ideal types existing in God belong more to the past in African cosmology as points of origination than in the future. So to make his perception of time more African he reverses Augustine's construct and makes the pre-existent past a hope to be recovered in its perfected form, hence hindsight as foresight. This is what makes sense in our claim that we learn from experience. What is more, it is this insight that allows us to say that the future will be better.

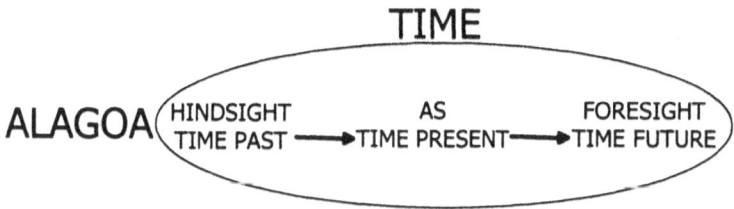

Here Alagoa shares the notion of the totality and complexity of time with Augustine but differs from him on the basis of the point of origination of time consciousness. Following the Alagoan typology, Augustine's *City of God* as the ideal City would then be the pre-existent City of God which was and has been from which the city of man is an imperfect type. For Alagoa therefore, the pre-existent City of God as hindsight serves as the hope of the future. Alagoa also notes that such a focus on the past can only be achieved from the locus in the present, powerfully influenced by expectations of the future and considerations of the moment. This introduces other forms of time consciousness which can be represented as follows:

(a)

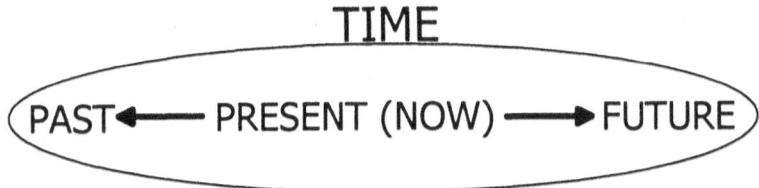

Here the present is tending towards the past in remembrance and at the same time tending towards the future in anticipation. Thus we say that both the past as remembered and the future as projected depend on the present.

(b)

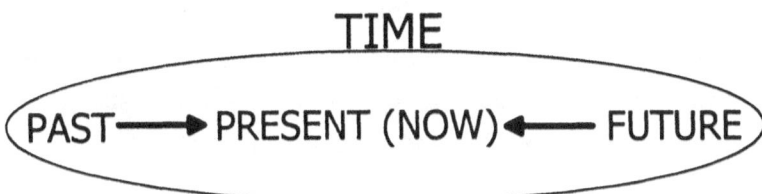

Without the past and the future there can be no present. Both the past and the future as inseparable entities constitute the present. Thus the present depends on both the past and the future. Given these various levels of time consciousness Alagoa admits that time remains a very complex subject in African time consciousness.[22] This complexity is also found in Ibibio time consciousness where the word **mkpong** is used to capture both the Past and the Future.

The Concept of *Mkpong* in Ibibio Time Consciousness

The dialogue below captures an aspect of Ibibio time consciousness.
Question: Nso usen ke ekedi? (When did you come?)
Answer: *mkpong* (Yesterday)
(What day did you come?)
Question: Nso usen ke edidi? (When will you come?)
Answer: *mkpong* (Tomorrow)
(What day will you come?)
The first question is past regarding and the answer *mkpong* (meaning yesterday). The second question is future regarding and yet the answer is the same *mkpong* (meaning tomorrow). Thus in Ibibio time awareness; *mkpong* can mean yesterday (referring to the past) or tomorrow (referring to the future). There are no different words for past and future. To talk about distant past or distant future you can only refer to them as **edem mkpong**. The meaning can only be understood in context whether one is talking about past or future.

Similarly, the word **mfin** (today) or **idahami** (now) can mean both past and future. For example
1. Question: *Nso usen ke ekedi?* (When did you come?)
   Answer: *mfin* (today)
   (What day did you come?)
2. Question: *Nso usen ke edidi?* (When will you come?)
   Answer: *mfin* (today)
   (What day will you come?)
3. Question: *Nso usen ke ekedi?* (When did you come?)
   Answer: *idahami* (now)
   (What day did you come?)

4. Question: *Nso usen ke edidi?* (When will you come?)
   Answer: *idahami* (now)
   (What day will you come?)

The first question is past regarding and the answer is **mfin** (today). The second is future regarding yet the answer is the same *mfin* (today). The third question is past regarding and the answer is *idahami* (now). The fourth question is future regarding yet the answer is the same *idahami* (now). One may wish to ask what the difference is between *mfin* (today) and *idahami* (now). *Mfin* refers to today (present) as between morning and evening of the same day whereas *idahami* (now) refers to today (present) as the now moment. This sameness of answer both for the past regarding situation and for the future regarding situation portrays the complexity of time consciousness in most African world views. This is what Augustine also realized when he concluded that he knows what time is but when he wants to explain it to someone; he does not know it anymore.[23]

With the notion of time seen in St Augustine of Targaste, confirmed by the Ibibio notion of time and collaborated by Alagoa's hindsight and foresight, it is definitely not the case that African concept of time has no sense of future as was insinuated by John Mbiti when he reflected on the African concept of time in his work, *African Religions and Philosophy*.[24] Rather, as John A.A. Ayoade has said of Africans of Yoruba extraction, they do have a perspective of time-future that extends beyond the end of this life to an after life.[25] What Mbiti failed to capture is the degree of complexities in the interrelation between past and present on the one hand

and past and future on the other, and similarly the relationship between present and past on the one hand and present and future on the other.

As a way of coming to terms with these complexities, Alagoa seeks to recover the African notion of time in its orality through the oral text such as proverbs and in these he found flexibility in the conceptions. Using selected Nembe proverbs he shows how time present falls between time future and time past.

1. Irusi / Igoin di (Laziness breeds poverty).[26]
2. Dorigha kana / fun tangha (An unwoven basked cannot carry away dirt).[27]
3. Egberi gbabo / din mindi gbagha (A story teller does not tell about another tide (season).[28]

According to Alagoa, text 1 above draws from the past in that its moral validity lies in experience. Yet the maxim itself is intended for application in the present, to save people from falling into destitution in the future. Text 2, too, is a present-oriented truism derived from past experience, used to persuade to action in the present to provide for the future. Text 3 affirms the primacy of the present over memory of the past. The present therefore becomes the touchstone by which the past is validated.[29]

Alagoa on Knowledge

On his epistemological bearing, one proverb summarizes his theory of knowledge. He states it thus: "What an old man sees sitting down, a young man cannot see standing."[30] In his explanation of this proverb he said that:

> The African image of an elder who sits contrasted with the standing young man symbolizes just such a possibility of wisdom arising from a long perspective of experience in the past, as opposed to a view limited to the recent past ... It is understood that the standing youth does not in fact command a better view. The point of the proverb being that exact vision of the present reality is not all, that experience of the past is required to interpret the present.[31]

Here Alagoa presents himself as a realist who bases his knowledge on experience. The experience of what was seen, of what is being experienced today and of what will be experienced tomorrow forms the basis of all knowledge. However, it should be noted that this theory of knowledge is based on Alagoa's philosophy of history and the methodology of the historiography of oral history. That is why the image of the seated elder who has the wealth of experience is very important in accessing and assessing knowledge. One thing that should also be noted is that Alagoa's notion of experience is not exactly like that of the empiricists in the tradition of George Berkeley where the *esse est percipii* is popularized. Rather it is a notion of perception which apart from sense experience allows for intuitive awareness, memory and anticipation as forms of experience.

The Moral Content of Alagoa's Philosophy of History

It is only the good or heroic past which is remembered that gives hope for the future. He therefore calls on the Niger Delta people to be positivistic both in their memory and in their thinking. For, according to him this is the only way they can stay focused and develop the present positively and thereby guarantee a better future. The proverb texts 1-3 above connote advocacy for hard work, foresight, and determination to change a bad history into something better.

The Philosopher as a Social Critic

One of the functions of a philosopher in the Socratic tradition is to serve as the conscience of the society by constantly raising questions that prick the conscience of the society. E.J. Alagoa, in his years of public life has done a great deal in this area. He wrote:

> Accountability has been all but absent in the governance of the Niger Delta region as it has largely been of the Nigerian nation in the last several decades. Local governments have been grievously guilty of misappropriation of all funds released to them from the federal government. Similarly, the state governments in the region have not carried out development on any scale close to the sums received from the federal government, inadequate as we note these payments to have been. The lack of accountability increases tension and

instability, since the youth are unemployed, and see injustice at every turn. The present circumstances of the Niger Delta: neglect by federal, state, and local governments, destruction of natural resources by oil extraction, gas flaring and pollution, and other numerous evidence of social and political injustice. The populations left in abject poverty cannot but remain restive and openly violent on every occasion.

On the issue of phenomenal proliferation of new churches, Alagoa notes that these followers of churches do not consider as their primary goal the matter of "where we will spend eternity" but that they are searching for a god who can solve their human problems. He writes:

> If one takes account of the phenomenal proliferation of new churches ... the primary issue with many attendants to churches and mosques would appear to be, how to relieve their present suffering on earth. Nigerians would appear to be this-worldly rather than other-worldly. Nigerians are religious, and place God unambiguously at the top of the pantheon of gods, but do not place all their trust in this world on God for their fate in this world. They are all too willing to go and serve other gods on earth, including the gods of money, success, and power.[33]

Here Alagoa takes a critical review of Nigerians' apparent religiosity. It is more the drive of material gains that makes a lot of Nigerians run after so many churches with the hope that they will find one that meets their earthly needs. It is the church that works whether through the power of Beelzebub or Satan they would care less provided it meets their existential needs. Alagoa sees this proliferation of churches not as evidence of faith in God but as exhibition of faithlessness and the quest for material gain.

Alagoa: a Philosophic Personality or a Virtuous Man

In his speech about who is and what he believes, and speaking within the rubrics of his hindsight as foresight, he says that he has come to realize that it was the foresightedness of grandmother many years ago in teaching him that "material goods are inferior in value to good works, a good name, a good heart and spiritual endowments," that have made him who he is today. This hindsight is very much in keeping with his philosophy that today is yesterday's foresight. In the same reasoning he admits that all processes of developing a personal philosophy of life was inevitably influenced by the friends and colleagues he has/had in his life journey. In other words, his past is the organizing principle of what and who he is today and tomorrow.

In his basic convictions he had this to say:

> I believe in loyalty to grass roots entities from the village up to the Nigerian nation. I believe that commitment to the Nigerian nation can

derive from strong attachment to specific environments. Such communities provide evidence of tolerance of neighbouring and distant communities which, in practice, develop relationships of mutual understanding and viable feelings of interdependence. I believe that our loyalty to the Nigerian nation can be based on such concrete practical roots of human understanding, tolerance and interdependence. I believe that a degree of consciousness of the past, and therefore, a regard for the future consequences of our present actions among leaders and people, will make a difference in the quality of governance in the nation. I believe that getting on in life means competition against my own personal weakness in order to achieve excellence; it does not mean a debilitating rat race against my peers.[34]

What he says he believes is true of who he is and what he does. His belief in the grassroots has made him return to Nembe in search of its oral history to authenticate who he is and who the Nembe people are. It is this consistency of being which defines and authenticates his person (in the Socratic tradition) that has made Alagoa: the Philosopher.

Conclusion

Alagoa's Hindsight as Foresight has emerged as a profound philosophical construct that allows for a new historiography wherein oral history is seen and understood as a pre-eminent form of history. This has come to be seen as a better form of history because it provides evidence for why it is told. Alagoa chose to develop an African historiography on oral history because it is true hindsight that is the hope of the future.

What is more, Hindsight as Foresight serves as an epistemological construct that provides the foundation for all forms of knowledge. It has provided a framework for the establishment of the metaphysics of time. As seen in the text, it has also served as the groundwork for ethical conduct. Who else can have this deep insight to reality except the philosopher?

3

Alagoa, Oral Tradition and the Multi-Method Approach

Robin Horton

Since this gathering is an occasion for celebrating our relations with E.J. the man as well as for celebrating the achievements of Alagoa the academic, I make no apology for starting on a personal note. As the British would say, E.J. and I go back a long way—forty-plus years to be mathematical. I still take pride in the small part I played, along with others, in getting him across from Unilag to Ibadan in 1966. But I am only emboldened to talk about it by his subsequent multiple repayments of this little debt. As a dissident and whistle-blower by temperament, I have been subjected during my time in Nigeria to periodic calls of "Horton must go!", especially immediately prior to and during my years at Uniport. And after most of such calls, it has been E.J. who has moved quietly but effectively to ensure my survival. So much for this E.J. the loyal friend. Now for Alagoa the innovative historian.

    &   &   &   &

Here, let me begin with my perceptions of the state of historical studies in Nigeria when I first took up an academic career in the country.

When I joined the old University of Ife (now Obafemi Awolowo University) in 1962, I found myself at the back gate of the Ibadan University campus, and was soon in contact with its academic life. In those days, Ibadan was a world centre for scholars interested in West Africa, and its History Department was one of the most highly respected institutions. In the light of my own academic background, however, I came to see the Nigerian History School as somewhat limited in methodology and scope.

As I saw it, the data-base of the School consisted of contemporary written documents set down in either Arabic or European script; documents that were studied largely within the confines of libraries or archives. This limitation of the data-base seemed to me to have a number of consequences; some direct, some less direct but nonetheless real. The most obvious of such consequences was the restriction of historical coverage of the West African region to the areas and periods for which contemporary written documents were available. This, of course, left a huge gap, not only in the broad swathe of territory between the coastal and savanna zones, but also in earlier periods in the history of both these zones. Amongst less direct consequences were: an emphasis on the history of centralised states and an almost total neglect of that of non-centralised polities; and emphasis on the lives and activities of individual poetical and religious leaders rather than on overall patterns of economic and socio-political organisation; and a neglect of many aspects of pre-Muslim, pre-Christian culture, especially the religious. This, I suggest, was the situation when Alagoa arrived in Ibadan to take up an appointment in the Institute of African Studies.

Alagoa came into Nigerian academic history with an unusual background. For the first ten years of his life, he had grown up in a small rural community remote from centres of modern formal education. The community was endowed with a purely oral culture, rich in narrative both historical and fictional and in historically allusive songs, drum praises and material symbols. All of this rich fare presented the past as an essential guide to living and achieving fulfilment in the present.

At the age of ten, however, he was transferred to the first of a succession of centres where he was faced with the challenge of catching up in an entirely different educational system; one from which he had been an absentee all through its supposedly crucial early years. In the event, he climbed brilliantly through the system to his first degree, overtaking in the process most of his contemporaries who had been in it from the beginning.

A good part of his curriculum through this period was historical. But it was history learned from books and through teaching based on written documents and books; and although he demonstrated mastery of this type of work, his heart was not wholly in it. The source material seemed cold and dry by comparison with the oral traditions, songs, drum praises and symbols which had enriched and shaped his childhood.

His own inclinations, however, were not to be fulfilled in the immediate aftermath of his first degree. Thus although he had caught the eye of Kenneth Dike, then the doyen of Nigerian historians and a Niger Delta specialist, the latter secured him his first professional job, not in a history department, but in the National Archives—an institution in which he found himself still immersed in the world of purely written sources, and with little chance to pursue his own research dreams. Before long, however, Dike came to his rescue, securing him a Carnegie Fellowship in the Programme of Comparative Tropical History in the University of Wisconsin at Madison. It was here he came under the supervision of Jan Vansina, a mentor who was to be a powerful influence on his latter intellectual development.

Vansina, a historian-cum-anthropolgist by training, had been one of the pioneers in exploring the historical implications of African oral traditions, working in particular with data from Ruanda, Burundi and Zaire.[1] He was delighted to find in Alagoa, not only a fellow devotee of oral sources, but one whose most formative years had been spent in the bosom of oral culture. He encouraged him in doctoral work which focused on the history of the Niger Delta—history based largely on oral tradition.

When Alagoa returned to Nigeria after the completion of his doctorate, he quickly secured an appointment as lecturer in the Unilag History Department. However, although he found the departmental atmosphere pleasant, he had a heavy teaching load and little prospect of time and money with which to follow up his Niger Delta research.

A renewed opportunity to pursue his central interest came when, transferring to the University of Ibadan, he joined, not the History Department but the Institute of African Studies. The Institute, at that time, was a multi-disciplinary unit whose membership covered such diverse fields as linguistics, oral literature, comparative ethnography, archaeology and palynology. It was also a unit committed primarily to research rather than to teaching. Here, he was free from any attempt to impose the kind of limitation then prevalent in Nigerian history departments; free to carry on with work on Niger Delta oral tradition that he had begun as PhD student under Vansina.

Much of his work, of course, involved explicit requests directed to carefully chosen informants for oral recitations concerning specific aspects of their personal, lineage or communal pasts. However, it also involved systematic recording of songs, drum-names and symbolic objects in ancestral shrines, all of which were triggers for historical exegesis. Such work required long absences from the comforts of the Ibadan campus, and took him to some of the less accessible parts of the Niger Delta. In those days when the East-West Road and mobile phones had scarcely even been dreamed of, his prolonged disappearances caused considerable anxiety amongst both family and colleagues. This was especially so during the Civil War, when refusing to be daunted by the hostilities, he continued his researches only just outside the western boundary of rebel-held territory.

One thing Alagoa soon came to realise was the orthographically accurate transcription of oral materials recorded on tape in the field quickly threatened to take up so much of a scholar's time that he had none left for analysis and interpretation of his data. Clearly, the only possible remedy for this situation was responsible delegation; and together with his linguistic colleagues, Bob Armstrong and Kay Williamson, he made a valuable attempt to apply this remedy. Thus between them, the three scholars managed to recruit, train and give regular employment to a corps of specialist transcribers whose skills covered a variety of southern Nigerian languages. Members of this corps were people, despite their modest educational qualifications, deeply dedicated to putting their several cultural heritages on record. When Alagoa and Williamson moved down to help found the University of Port Harcourt, those of the corps whose skills related to the Niger Delta languages happily followed them. The services of this little group at Uniport excited the envy of several African Studies centres overseas. Indeed, I even came across an attempt (happily unsuccessful) to lure at least one member across the Atlantic.

Having taken a creative lead in expanding the scope of narrative resources to include the oral alongside the written, Alagoa went on to reach out to members of other disciplines that used non-narrative sources in the reconstruction of the past, urging them to join historians in a common enterprise. Such disciplines included archaeology, palynology, comparative ethnography and historical linguistics. Several of those concerned were already at hand at the Ibadan Institute; and they in turn passed on the message to close associates of the Institute. Nor was he content with mere methodological reflections on modes of co-operation between History and these other disciplines—reflections which by themselves might have had little practical effect. Rather, he gave them a specific target area on which to direct their combined efforts: none other, of course, than his beloved Niger Delta. In the post-Civil-War period, moreover, he personally led several inter-disciplinary teams to the region; often, once again, to areas remote and difficult to access. By guiding them in to a definite common target, he forced members of these teams to think hard about the specifics of multi-method co-operation. I believe these efforts encouraged a new direction in Nigerian historical thinking: a new direction whose implications ranged far beyond the Niger Delta.

Students and scholars wishing to get an over-view of the contributions outlined above could usefully start by reading two publications: first, Alagoa's *History of the Niger Delta,* in which he explores the potential of oral tradition as source material for the history of the region; and second, his co-edited volume, *The Early History of the Niger Delta*, in which he and several of his collaborators explore the potential of the multi-method approach to that history.[2]

Despite his successes in the practical implementation of his historiographic vision, Alagoa has also experienced some serious frustrations of his efforts. Thus after some years of useful work at the University of Port Harcourt, the corps of transcribers which he had helped to set up was disbanded under circumstances which I can only describe as obscure. Indeed, when I asked around for the reasons behind this puzzling action, the most I could get by way of explanation was that the powers of those days had decided that the corps was an unnecessary innovation brought in by the 'Old Guard', and as such was ripe for disbanding. Wow! Another instance of such frustration was the chronic opposition to his efforts toward the establishment at Uniport of an Institute of Niger Delta Studies. Such an institute would have provided an ideal forum for furthering his multi-method research programme. Indeed, by involving not only History and the social sciences, but also the natural sciences, it would have done much to set the peoples of the region in their remarkable natural context. Given the location of the University, moreover, this would have been a highly appropriate place in which to put such a unit. Once again, the circumstances of the blockage remain obscure. Perhaps the most one can say at present, both about this and the previous case, is that dreams of Alagoa (and indeed of other members of the 'Old Guard') have suffered considerably down the years from people who came to Uniport to be, as they wrongly thought they would be, one-eyed kings in the kingdom of the blind. Let me leave it for some future historians of our university to bell these cats in retrospect. Meanwhile, it is consoling to see that what did not come to fruition at Uniport looks like doing so at the Niger Delta University next door. There, with Alagoa as Chairman of Council, an Institute of Niger Delta Studies is already on the books; and one may hope soon to see a transcription corps as part of its establishment. Whatever the future of developments at the institutional level, moreover, one can safely say that, at the level of individual scholarship and informal co-operation, Alagoa's work has played a key part, not just in advancing the study of the Niger Delta past, but also more generally, in helping to broaden the methodological base of Nigerian academic historians.

As those of you who have followed Alagoa down the multi-method road will surely be aware already, the road is by no means a smooth one. Thus on the one hand, it has led to a greatly enlarged vision of the possibilities of historical coverage of the West African region both in space and time. On the other hand, however, it has presented the scholar with a whole host of new problems. Reverting to Anglo-American idiom, one might go so far as to say that it has opened a whole new can of worms! This is particularly the case where different types of source material suggest dramatically different historical interpretations. For instance, oral tradition and contemporary written documents can suggest highly divergent versions of key historical events. Again, ethnographic data may suggest that a particular oral tradition is not so much the deposit of past events as a charter legitimating the current *status quo*. Yet again, devotees of oral tradition may find their narratives of origin, migration and dispersal challenged by historical linguists operating in the light of their own brand of non-narrative data. In quite a few such cases, it would seem that oral tradition, despite being the most humanly compelling of all historical sources, is very much under siege.

Some African historians, taking oral-traditional history as central to the cultural identity of the continent and its peoples, seem to see scepticism about it as part of a broader Euro-American dismissiveness of things African. Such scholars tend to suggest that this scepticism will evaporate as African historians take over with increasing self-confidence from their Euro-American counterparts. To me however, this seems too simplistic. Thus on one hand, annoyance with the biting critiques of some foreign methodologists such as Henige[3] should not tempt us to forget that one of the pioneer advocates of the historical value of African oral traditions was the Belgian Vansina. On the other hand, moreover, we have among African historical scholars not only whole-hearted advocates of the historical value of this source, but also whole-hearted (albeit less vocal) sceptics. With regard to the latter, the negative experience of one of the brightest of my old students still sticks vividly in my mind. This student, in his application for admission to the History doctoral programme of a well-known Nigerian University (not Uniport!), announced his desire to write a thesis based on oral traditions of his birthplace. He was duly admitted, but only after being diverted to a topic based on contemporary written documents. The reason given was that the department concerned had no one capable of supervising such a thesis! When I recounted this incident to Alagoa, he capped my story with a similar incident involving one of his own academic protégés. These and other instances suggest that there are still reputable Nigerian historians who stick to contemporary written records as their sole source of evidence, and who do so, amongst other reasons, because of a continuing general scepticism about oral tradition as historical source. The long and short of all this, I think, is that the major methodological and theoretical issues at stake transcend the specifics of the indigenous or non-indigenous origins of those debating them, and would still persist as topics, either of overt dispute or of silent but obdurate disagreement, even were Nigerian or African historiography to be entirely in the hands of Nigerian or African historians.

Nor, it seems to me, would the persistence of such dispute and disagreement sound the death-knell of oral tradition as an historical source. Here, perhaps, I may be permitted to cite the support two of my own historical excursions using the multi-method approach: an earlier one focusing on the Yoruba 'holy city' of Ile-Ife.[4] and a later one focusing on the origins and dispersals of the Ijọ-speaking peoples of the Niger Delta.[5] In both cases, I took the fullest possible account, not only for extant oral traditions, but also of linguistic and archaeological evidence. In both cases, I found discrepant historical indications, even within oral traditions themselves, not to speak of those between the oral traditions and the non-narrative sources. In both cases, moreover, I had to tinker a good deal with oral traditions in order to square them with non-narrative evidence: sorting out earlier from later versions; in some places weighting minority against majority versions; in others choosing a particular version but excising portions of it. In both cases, nonetheless, I found that my historical conclusions had to include elements at least of the contents of the relevant narratives. Had I been totally dismissive of such narratives, I should have missed vital clues to historical reality.

The lesson I draw from these first-hand experiences is three-fold. First, that in many or perhaps even in most cases where oral tradition is used as one amongst several types of source material in the multi-method approach, there will be problems of discrepant historical indications that will have to be squarely faced by the researcher. Second, that the character and scale of the problems will vary widely from case to case. Third, that oral tradition will nonetheless continue to be an indispensable source for reconstruction of the West African past.

At this point, let us round off our discussion by returning to Alagoa; for in large measure, it is *his* innovative efforts that have opened up this field of endeavour and controversy for his colleagues in the Nigerian History School. Ironically, these very efforts appear to constitute a source of tensions within his own thought. Thus on the one hand, there is his deep faith in oral tradition as a prime source of historical truth—a faith arguably grounded in the intense and formative experiences of his childhood. Yet on the other, there is a strong commitment to the multi-method approach with its frequent challenges to such tradtion—a commitment grounded in his later fertile interactions with members of disciplines other than History.[6] However, as some of us who have experienced similar tensions in this and other fields of endeavour can testify, they need not be disabling. Rather, they can keep us alert and intellectually restless. Indeed, I am tempted to compare tensions with the sand grains that irritate oysters and provoke them into secreting pearls. Alagoa has already secreted many such pearls for us; and we may hope that continued irritation will provoke him into secreting more in the years to come.

    &   &   &   &

Thanks in considerable part to Alagoa, we now have several members of the younger generation of Nigerian historians who are equipped and ready to expand the scope of their work through the multi-method approach. Not surprisingly, moreover, some of these are targeting the Niger Delta as their field of operation. Sadly, though, conditions in the region are at present far from propitious for academic field-work. The financial spill-over from oil exploration to the local communities affected has brought wide-spread conflict at both intra-communal and inter-communal levels. The frustration and despair of unemployed youths has made them a ready source of cannon-fodder in the prosecution of such conflict. Again, the contrast between the oil-induced devastation of many parts of the region and oil-fuelled affluence of Abuja has given a perverse but understandable sense of justification and even legitimacy to the oil-bunkerers and their cohorts. And woe betide anyone who inadvertently strays into the midst of their operations. All this has made for a general security situation ill-suited to the aspirations of the new generation of would-be Niger Delta historians. Coming to specifics, one can say yet more. Thus the long-standing use of oral traditional histories to justify claims to territorial sovereignty and authority seems about to spin out of control. Whatever the constraints in earlier times (and I for one believe there were such constraints), greedy, ambitious individuals and groups will now say almost anything about their past in the hope of getting their claims to financial reward accepted by oil companies and/or government. Again, if an archaeologist wants to excavate a suspected key site, and takes pains to secure permission from what he assumes is the relevant authority, he is likely to be challenged and blocked almost immediately by a rival claimant to such authority. Yet again, linguists are apt to be attacked for their scholarly conclusions about language relationships, when these do not tally with the assimilatory or separatist ambitions of the leaders of ethnic groups—ambitions bearing once again on oil-related financial benefits.

Confronted with this depressing scene, Alagoa, as usual, has put his money where his mouth is. He has published several books and pamphlets in which he suggests how the insights of a historian can be drawn upon in the search for a way back to sanity for the peoples of the region.[7] He has also been moving quietly behind the scenes to persuade regional intellectual and political leaders of the usefulness of his ideas. I shall leave it to other contributors to our symposium to say more about these interventions in contemporary political debate. Meanwhile, let me join them in wishing him success in his elder-statesmanly role. At the same time, we must urge him to keep a big place in his life for the more purely academic side of things. Unsolved problems still abound, with regard both to the multi-method approach and to the specifics of Niger Delta history; and his continued academic inspiration in both these areas will long be needed.

4

Alagoa as Pioneer of Oral Tradition and Oral History in the Niger Delta

Nkparom C. Ejituwu
and
John H. Enemugwem

Abstract

Historians cherish the great innovations brought by Alagoa into the historical discipline in Nigeria. An examination of his work has revealed three important contributions to Niger Delta historiography. These are his pioneering efforts in the use of oral traditions, oral history and ethnographic data in reconstructing the past. From here he advocated for the recognition of oral data as archives in Africa and the Third World. These innovations constitute the discourse of this paper.

Introduction

Born on Friday 14 April, 1933 at Nembe (Brass) in the Niger Delta, Ebiegberi Joe Alagoa, spent over thirty years teaching, researching and publishing in universities within and outside Nigeria. In this period, he contributed to the development of historical writing in the Niger Delta in particular and Nigeria in general. As one of the founding archivists of the National Archives, he assisted Nigerian historians in the use of archival materials. According to Agiri (1998: 5), he demonstrated it by using archival evidence to prepare the manuscript of his work, *The Small Brave City State: A History of Nembe (Brass) in the Niger Delta* (1964).

Nonetheless, Alagoa was one of the brains behind the introduction of African history as a subject in the Nigerian educational syllabus. His book, *Jaja of Opobo: The Slave Who Became a King* (1970), was intended specifically for the teaching of history at the primary and secondary school levels. Since his emphasis was on decolonization of African history, he published over 40 works as books, chapters in books, mimeographs and articles in scholarly journals world-wide and helped in the training of professional African historians for this assignment. This paper focuses on his role in the development of history writing in the Niger Delta region.

Pioneer of Oral Tradition in the Niger Delta

Oral Tradition has been a part of Niger Delta culture before Alagoa's birth. But it was hardly recognised by the outside world. Alagoa (1981: 194), saw oral traditions as valid historical documents. Oral traditions, being information from the distant past about life patterns of the people include events, oral literature such as proverbs, poetry, riddles, prose narratives and music. Like written history, oral traditions entail a systematic recalling of the past as it affects the present and plans for the future. Isichei (1982) credited the Niger Delta with a massive literature and Afigbo (1993: 40-43) accorded the region and the North African coast the distinction of being the pioneer of African places of scholarship. Oral tradition is the unified mode of historical consciousness in the Niger Delta. Information about its past comes from oral sources.

According to Ejituwu (2004: 2), Dike and Jones entered the historical field before Alagoa. While Dike's *Trade and Politics in the Niger Delta* (1956) used more of archival materials and less of oral tradition, Jone's *Trading States of the Oil Rivers* (1963) is the reverse. Dike and Jones are remembered for laying the foundation for the decolonization of African history. Dike pioneered the use of archival materials in reconstructing the Nigerian past. But the external evidence of archival records he used in his reconstruction could not give him enough facts going deep into the internal history of the people. As a result, he and Jones could not cover the entire Niger Delta in their work.

Alagoa entered the field at this juncture. He studied oral traditions from his infancy. In the view of Agiri (1985: 5), Alagoa was below the age of nine when he began to observe his grandmother telling oral traditions. This deepened his interest in using it as evidence of the past. He was the first African doctoral student to be trained in oral historical methodology in the United States of America under Jan Vansina, the scholar who devised a method of salvaging the past of preliterate societies. Within this period, Vansina's work, *Oral Tradition: A Study in Historical Methodology* (1965) was published.

After training, Alagoa exhibited the fact that "the measure of a man is in what he did with his training". His pioneering efforts in making the Ijọ oral traditions a major historical source emanated from his doctoral research in 1964. The end product was *A History of the Niger Delta: An historical interpretation of Ijọ oral traditions* (1972). It covered every Ijọ community in the Delta. It was not only an attempt to reconstruct a history of the Delta from their traditions but also the first historical work of the Niger Delta Ijọ using the internal evidence of the people. This established Alagoa as the pioneer of oral tradition in the Niger Delta.

Alagoa deviated from Dike and Jones and carefully went for the custodians of oral traditions in every Ijọ community. In recording traditions from his informants, he also documented their biographical data. This innovation guides budding historians of the Niger Delta who accept all forms of traditions as sources of African history. He enjoined his students to subject every bit of oral data to critical analysis and interpretation, to collect and reconstruct family and lineage traditions first before attempting to create "the general patterns, trends and development of Ijọ history" (Alagoa, 1972: 1-5). Through such a method, he traced the origin, migrations and settlement history of every Ijọ clan from the Western Delta to the Eastern Delta.

The traditions were not without limitations. First, oral traditions give only relative and not absolute time-depth. Second was the problem of loss of detail which comes from weak memory. Alagoa (1972: 3) confirmed that "they [the oral traditions] really refer to only a fraction of the history". He also detected the unreliability of some informants using oral tradition to make political claims. In "Dating Ijọ Oral traditions", Alagoa (1972: 5 and 1976: 19-22) first determined the reliability of relative chronology "from a detailed analysis of comparative traditions." After this, he converted into absolute chronology. Being a tentative estimate, it is only archaeological dating that can validate it. For loss of details and political charter, he collected variant versions of oral traditions and used the common denominator. These methods became the norm in the Niger Delta (Alagoa 1972: 4-5).

Three conclusions flow from Alagoa's work in the Niger Delta. First, no matter the limitations, oral traditions penetrate farther into the distant past than the written data. Second, it provides a comprehensive coverage of the precolonial history of the Ijọ communities. Third, it is the internal evidence of the people and as such gives the most authentic account of their past. But Alagoa continued to search for other ways to overcome the limitations of the oral traditions.

Alagoa and the Use of Ethnographic Data

Alagoa (1981: 201) defines ethnography as festivals, rituals, economic and political activities of the people. It is also one of the disciplines required to interprete oral traditions. The other two are archaeology and linguistics. He has always cautioned his history students that no historian should rely on one evidence but on a combination of several sources. Each of them has its merits and demerits and historians are after the merits which are reliable for reconstructing the past.

Ethnographic data, like the best archives, came into being independent of history and provide good support for oral traditions. Vansina (1968: 97-124) calls ethnographic data artefacts, customs, the belief system and culture which testify to ways of life of a people in the past. As a result, Alagoa saw it as additional historical evidence which complements oral traditions and good for reconstructing the past.

Alagoa used ethnographic records in the following manner. First, he collected oral data on the formal traditions of the communities of study. Second, he invokes the ethnographic records to check its reliability, complement the information from oral tradition and resolve the problems associated with the latter. For instance, ethnographic data is the means of extending human memory. This solves the problems of weak memory and political charter. It gives the field worker a wider view of the people's traditions as a document of their past in the present. Through it, the historian searches for historical data in all aspects of the people's life. Alagoa's use of ethnographic documents in his Niger Delta history has made the historians of oral tradition to see it as part of their routine work. Every bit of ethnographic documents including masquerades and drumbeats are imbued with meaning. Alagoa (1981: 200) sees this method as looking outside to other bodies of oral data. Without it, no historical reconstruction in oral civilization can be complete.

Alagoa: Advocate of Oral Traditions as Archives in Africa and Pioneer of Oral History in the Niger Delta

Alagoa's usage of oral traditions and ethnographic data in reconstructing the past enabled him to see them as archives in Africa. Archives are not only repositories devoted solely to written data. but to him, documents are equated with history as things that come from the past as evidence of the past (Alagoa 1981:193-202). In the light of this definition, archival documents are impartial and reliable sources for historical construction. Since written records are inadequate, Alagoa advocated that oral records that support it should be processed and preserved as archives in Africa.

Alagoa also pioneered the use of oral history. Alagoa and Williamson (1981: 167-227) documented the oral history of the Anglo-Nembe War of 1895, following Alagoa's earlier work, *The Akassa Raid, 1895* (1960). This is a rare feat.

Conclusion

The paper discusses Alagoa's contributions to the development of historical writing in the Niger Delta. Although Dike and Jones preceded him, he made advances in oral tradition and oral history. His *History of the Niger Delta* (1972) is his definitive interpretation of Ijọ oral traditions. Alagoa is the pioneer of oral tradition, oral history and the use of ethnographic data in the Niger Delta.

5

Keeping the Faith

Ebiegberi Joe Alagoa

There are several constituencies to which I must give an account of how well or ill I have kept the faith.

In writing the local history of communities one feels bound to keep faith with the ancestors and the elders who had passed on their knowledge of the folk. None of the work I have done has been without controversy, although I have rarely engaged in discourse with my critics. The only instance was the opportunity afforded me by Chief Ebitimi Banigo Ogbulu to hold a symposium with violent critics in Okpoama, prior to the publication of the book, *The People of the Fish and Eagle: A History of Okpoama in the Eastern Niger Delta* (1995). In all of that memorable encounter (Alagoa, 2001: 91-102), my confidence lay in my faithful interpretation of the evidence of my reliable, mainly departed, informants. And eventually, my commitment to keep faith with the venerable ancestors.

In the course of training for the profession of historian, and in the course of my practice of the craft of history, I have been inspired by a small group of teachers, colleagues, and students. These people have challenged me to do better and aspire to excellence.

I cannot claim to have reached the standards set for me by my teachers or indicated to me by my critical colleagues and students, but remain grateful to them for pointing me to the sky I was unable to reach. I believe they assisted me to rise slightly above ground level. I restrain myself from naming names in a situation where so many have influenced me over so many years. I fear the consequences of missing out a crucial name.

Keeping faith with professional mentors and colleagues means keeping the faith of the code one has received from the profession of history. For me, keeping faith with the profession means: striving for objectivity as one may be able to approximate to it within the body of evidence available for the particular work at hand; accepting responsibility for any errors or limitations; standing ready to move forward in the light of new evidence or insights.

In the Ijọ creation myth, each Soul, as it leaves heaven to be born, recites to the Mother God, its own individual destiny according to its own will (Okara, 1958: 8-17). Keeping faith must therefore mean, in the final reckoning, the extent to which a life has fulfilled the destiny to which a Soul had committed itself to God in the beginning. By the age of three score and ten and over, one should care less with material success, and begin to draw closer to the rest of the Universe, becoming more and more spiritual and less and less material.

II

Yet the material body is important and we must take steps to sustain it. The Egyptians took extreme steps to preserve the dead in high pyramids and temples deep in the earth, a continuing testimony to their spirituality and wisdom. The Christian gospels record the efforts of Christ to raise the dead, and to rise from the dead in his material body into heaven. Nigerians attempt to keep this heritage in their obsessive desire to give their dead a "befitting burial", but do not take sufficient care to keep the living body in good health and welfare.

Life after retirement is a bleak one in Nigeria. To keep faith with life-long commitment to profession and perceived destiny, the way of the NGO consultancy and practice appears to be one viable route to follow. Onyoma Research has kept me in the path of research, writing and publication. Entry into publishing has opened avenues to returns from academic activity to support the inadequate pensions of the Nigerian public service. Research, publishing and consultancy in the area of my major academic interest, the Niger Delta region of Nigeria and its cultural links to the rest of the nation have proved quite fulfilling.

Retirement from direct public service employment in academics has meant greater engagement with community and other part-time public service appointments. Chieftaincy titles in the Niger Delta are more than honorific, and mean direct leadership and shepherding of groups of families, and membership of community Councils of Chiefs and the attendant social and political responsibilities.

The crises in the Niger Delta cease to be theoretical academic postulates, but practical problems to be addressed.

One approach to healing internal wounds, building unity, and moving the communities forward has been to lead the group of young people in Nembe Ibe Road Projects Group. This is a group composed of members from all communities within the Nembe-speaking area of Bayelsa State united by the positive focus on the construction of a network of roads, some proposed by government agencies since the 1960s! Unity and peace are seen as essential to achieve success, since pressure on state and federal government cannot be effective without the evidence of active public support. The elite have generally rallied. The traditional authorities support the programme, and the general public are enthusiastic and pray for success. It is the youth groups that remain to be integrated into the movement, and until that is achieved, no enduring victory can be won. But the degree of success achieved has already impressed state and federal government sufficiently to make public commitment to the cause of construction of a network of roads in this oil and gas producing location of the Niger Delta.

In the state setting, membership of the Bayelsa State Elders Consultative Council provides a forum for contributing ideas that stand a chance of reaching the ears of government. Service as Pro-Chancellor of the state's Niger Delta University, however, has proved less fulfilling than expected, but remains a way of influencing young academics along the lines of the pursuit of academic excellence. A second chance for such contribution is opening out in the decision of the Anglican Diocese of Niger Delta West to open its own institution, the Reverend D.O. Ockiya College of Theology and Management Sciences to whose Board I have been appointed Chairman.

Opportunities of limited service in the national cultural sector open out in the Slave Routes Project of the federal government under the leadership of Professor Ade Ajayi and the Intangible Cultural Heritage Project, both proposed by Unesco.

In the development of the history profession and the creation of national acceptance and relevance, support of the Historical Society of Nigeria remains central. Professor Ade Ajayi managed to get the federal government to return History into the syllabus at the Secondary School level, but the Historical Society of Nigeria is yet to get the policy implemented.

Our joint responsibility here is clear, to support the younger leaders of the Historical Society carry out its manifest duties to society, and point the younger generation of historians to higher standards of performance.

III

What hopes of success, what evidence of success, in these plans, projects and concepts for the future? We cannot precisely determine the shape of the future in the present, but we can attain peace of mind in the present through acting according to the dictates of our conscience. Keeping the faith must be a good guide for those of us far down the road to eternity.

And why this Concourse and to what end? It was the idea of my son David, and my colleagues in the University of Port Harcourt. My part was to suggest the names of possible contributors, my professional colleagues down the years from whom I have drawn most inspiration. The hope is that, we might, together, turn over in our minds our experiences of the Nigerian past. To what end? We must leave that to the judgment of posterity.

6

The Torch is Passed Over: Response to "Keeping the Faith"

Okon E. Uya

Introduction

Let me begin by expressing my profound thanks and gratitude to the organizers of this epoch making Concourse for the honour done me by their invitation to participate. May I also, on behalf of those who have been friends, teachers, academic associates, students and sincere well wishers of this significant monument to African historical scholarship, Professor E.J. Alagoa, or simply E.J.; as those of us close to him have gotten used to addressing him, congratulate him most warmly for attaining the enviable and divinely ordained age of seventy. That we have gathered in significant numbers and quality testifies to the wide ranging impact and influence of this capacity builder on the historical profession in Nigeria at one level. At yet another equally significant level, it testifies to the humane qualities of this gentleman-historian who has touched and shaped many lives in his sojourn on this earth by his example of patriotic service and commitment to excellence in whatever his hands have found to do. May God continue to preserve and prosper him for the benefit of our humankind.

2. Why Me?

When I got the letter inviting me to respond to the usually profound speech of E.J. on this occasion and to accept the torch on behalf of the generation of those succeeding Alagoa's, I began to wonder why I was so selected. Could it be because I come from a community, Oron in Akwa Ibom State, historically connected by rivers to E.J.'s Nembe in the eastern Niger Delta? This forced me to reflect on the possibility that but for western education, both of us would have been fishermen. Whether or not we would have succeeded as well as catchers of fish as we have been as fishers of men for the historical profession is better left to the imagination.

As a student at Hope Waddell Training Institution, Calabar and a member of the school's second eleven football team, we always played against Government College, Umuahia, where E.J. had his secondary education. Needless to say we almost always won in these matches, especially the one we played against the team in which my dear friend, late Ken Saro Wiwa, was a member.

Thirdly, both of us went to Nigeria's premier university, Ibadan, to which E.J. preceded me by a few years. E.J. was unfortunately condemned to the ranks of those who took the colonial degrees of the University of London in contrast to those of us who were fortunate to be proud pioneer holders of the certificates of the independent and autonomous University of Ibadan signed by our Dean, Professor J.F. Ade Ajayi, our

Oga Kpata Kpata, who is here with us in spirit. Besides, we both went to the University of Wisconsin and were fortunate to drink deep from the enviable pioneering activities of that prestigious American University in African history under the leadership of Jan Vansina, Philip Curtin, Suzane Miers, David Cronon and so on. Indeed, it was at Wisconsin that I was confronted and challenged by the reputation of E.J. as a most promising scholar of oral tradition methodology which Professor Jan Vansina never tired of talking about.

There is also the fact that both of us spent a substantial portion of our mature academic life in the Niger Delta, he at the University of Port Harcourt, and I at Calabar. Those who know the early histories of both will testify to the collaborative efforts of these institutions in sharing resources and academic expertise. Indeed, when Unical decided to build professorial houses at the time I served as Deputy Vice-Chancellor there, I simply drove to Port Harcourt where E.J., as Deputy Vice-Chancellor under Professor Donald Ekong, generously loaned us the drawings for the professorial houses they had earlier constructed. This saved the University of Calabar substantial amount of money which could have been spent on architectural and structural drawings.

Lastly, E.J. and I have generously shared our research efforts especially in matters of historical methodology over the years, I believe, more to my benefit than his. I must confess that other than Professor Adiele Afigbo, no other Nigerian historian has helped as much to sharpen my historical thinking as E.J. Alagoa.

What should be clear from the above for whatever reason I was chosen, I feel highly honoured to receive the torch of historical scholarship from one whose life and work have intersected and impacted on mine for nearly forty years. E.J., thank you for being such a wonderful friend, mentor and colleague all rolled into one for all these years.

What Are We Inheriting?

Gathered here are three generations of Nigerian historians represented by perhaps the doyen of each generation. Our mentor, Professor J.F. Ade Ajayi, represents the last stage of the first generation whose basic task was to rescue African history from the monumental distortions and falsehoods of Euro-American scholars who not only denied our historical heritage but also excluded us, by and large, from having played a significant role in their European drama of exploration, conquest, colonization, and administration of the continent. The pioneering works of this generation set new challenging directions for African historical studies in content and methodology. It was under their influence that Professor Alagoa began the journey that would take him to eminence in the writing of history.

Professor Alagoa properly belongs to the second generation, although his earliest publications appeared in the dying years of the first. The contribution of E.J.'s generation in the areas of the methodology of oral tradition historiography, inter-disciplinarity in the study of Africa history, and efforts at defining the character, meaning and philosophy of that history, properly so called, is no longer contestable, despite the false claim of some Euro-American scholars who condemn their impressive research output as "pathetically uncritical". Professor Adiele Afigbo, a significant member of this second generation, has aptly described the fulminations of these critics as "irrational scholarship". It is in recognition of E.J.'s monumental contribution to the shaping of the character of the scholarship of the period that he has appropriately been described as the doyen of oral history methodology and faithful application in the reconstruction of African history.

The third generation of Nigerian historians whose writings spanned the period from the late eighties through the nineties was expected, in the words of Afigbo, "to spend a little more time thinking about the meaning of the African past and its relevance to us today than they [were] spending ferreting out facts and still more facts about the past." This search for a usable African past capable of assisting African governments, if they care to listen, which confronts the problem of our catastrophe of governance remains a daunting challenge. Professor E.J. Alagoa has emerged as a major protagonist of this search for meaning and relevance in the study and writing of African history.

It is more important to stress that in a career spanning more than four decades, Professor E.J. Alagoa has contributed immensely to the study and practice of African history. His indelible marks are obvious particularly in the areas of the search for and production of source materials more in consonance with the African cultural experience; a more appropriate methodology for interpreting the historical evidences; the search for relevance and meaning; the production of worthy successors; and putting history and historical knowledge at the service of our community and nation building efforts. Our gathering here today is thus both a testimony to and recognition of how well he has succeeded as history teacher, researcher, writer, popularizer, and administrator. We thank God for giving us such a wonderful example of humility and total commitment in the service of history and a largely unappreciative nation.

The Challenge of Heritage

Fortunately, since scholars and academics can never retire from their calling which is life-long, we are today witnessing only the formal disengagement of Professor E.J. Alagoa from academic public service engagements. His life and work challenge us in several directions.

First is the challenge of the scholar to always identify with his roots and community. We note with satisfaction the fact that in retirement, E.J. is serving his Nembe community which has kept faith with him in generously sharing their traditions, as traditional ruler. We wish His Royal Highness success in his challenging job of being a catalyst for change and development for his people.

Second is the challenge of humility in service to a profession which not only nurtured but sustained his reputation for creative scholarship. We note that E.J. Alagoa's tenure as

President of the Historical Society of Nigeria was one of critical self-rediscovery for an association which had, by and large, become moribund.

Third is the challenge of excellence in creative scholarship even in the face of distracting noises from powerful and unsympathetic outsider colleagues. E.J. has today in fact given us the key for handling such detractors who will always abound for those who engage in cutting-edge scholarship, heresies of today will doubtless become the orthodoxies of tomorrow. That oral tradition methodology now occupies a respectable place in world historiography, indeed, the only universally acknowledged most important contribution of African history to world historiography, is a tribute to the consistency and doggedness of the E.J. Alagoas in the pursuit of the goals of their profession.

The enormous successes of E.J. Alagoa in the face of the frustrating circumstances in Nigeria for true professionals is cause for celebration. In this respect, one is reminded of the penury and indignities to which our pensioners are subjected by a largely unappreciative nation. We seem to have forgotten that the character of a nation is often judged by the care it extends to its vulnerable members: the aged, the sick, children and the handicapped. We are comforted that Professor Alagoa, as always, will turn this obstacle into a challenge and opportunity as he participates in the NGOs with which he is connected. In his profound words "by the age of three score and ten and over, one should care less with material success, and begin to draw closer to the rest of the universe, becoming more spiritual and less material" We know that surrounded by a loving family, E.J. will never allow the cares of this world deny him joy and peace of mind in retirement.

The momentous event also forces us to reflect on the Nigerian malady of retirement of people of experience still active in mind and body from participation in our universities. During my sojourn in the United States in the 1970s, I recall that Professor Merle Curti, and Professors Rayford Logan and Chancellor Williams, all eminent American historians, my colleagues at the University of Wisconsin, Madison and Howard University, Washington, DC respectively, were in their eighties. The full dimensions of this malady were clear to me when, in 2003, my dear friend, Professor Adiele Afigbo, who had earlier retired prematurely from the University of Nigeria, Nsukka was told that his contract with Abia State University, which incidentally he helped to establish as Commissioner for Education in old Imo State, could not be extended. Ironically, it was just at that time that Oxford University found him suitable for a fellowship to continue his research on the Atlantic Slave Trade in the Bight of Biafra. What a wasteful country that does not seem to appreciate the fact that committed academics never retire!

Conclusion

Finally, let me end by assuring Professor E.J. Alagoa, our man of the moment, that we, his friends, colleagues both senior and junior, former students and other collaborators are satisfied that he has paid his dues and has run the race with enormous faith and commitment. The greatest tribute we can pay to him as he enters this phase of reduced activities in his public service academic engagements is to reciprocate his faith by keeping the flag of historical scholarship flying.

Building on the foundation that he and his other contemporaries have so wonderfully laid, we must ensure that history is restored to its rightful place as a useful and usable discipline in our schools and other educational institutions. We must ensure that no historian, regardless of his place of origin, takes us back to the trenches in matters concerning the philosophy, nature, methodology, meaning, and utility of African history in our efforts at nation building. Not to do so will amount to betraying the faith that E.J. has in us to continue from where the pioneers are stopping. Admittedly, as E.J. has admonished, "we cannot precisely determine the shape of the future in the present", especially as historians are not given to prophesy. But there is enough evidence for us to conclude that the future of Nigerian, nay African, history is bright since we are committed to not allowing the labours of our teachers, mentors and friends like Professor E.J. Alagoa to have been in vain. We accept the torch of African historical scholarship and must ensure that the light does not go out in our hands. May the good Lord continue to give us the courage to be wise even in the midst of the confusion around us.

7

Professor E. J. Alagoa: A Cultural Nationalist

Bọlanlẹ Awẹ

I thank the Organizing Committee of this event for inviting me to it. Indeed I feel most highly honoured to have been asked to be part of this celebration. Professor E.J. Alagoa is someone I respect for many reasons; I have had the opportunity of working with him when he was in the Institute of African Studies of the University of Ibadan. I have therefore had the opportunity of watching him at close quarters and I can say without any iota of doubt that he is one of the most dedicated, and yet totally unassuming scholars that this country has produced, certainly in the field of history. He is painstaking in his search and yet has a knack of carrying his colleagues with him. I can also say that I have become a friend of the family, and Mercy, even though distance prevents us from interacting as closely as we would wish, remains my friend. Her warmth, openness, enthusiasm and energy captivated me on our first meeting and I do treasure the relationship. David was at the University of Loughborough with my son, Jide Awe, and that provides another generational link!

The topic, *Professor E.J. Alagoa: A Cultural Nationalist*, is one that should feature in any discussion of Alagoa, and will certainly suffuse any biography of him that would be written. It encapsulates what EJ stands for—his life, his works. The concept of nationalism and therefore being a nationalist can be interpreted in very many ways; it can mean different things to different people. In the Concise Oxford Dictionary, it means patriotic feeling, principles or efforts; it goes on to explain that its extreme form is marked by a feeling of superiority over other countries; it could also mean the advocacy of political independence for a particular country. In discussing Alagoa as a nations, we can quickly discard some of the elements encompassed by these meanings; certainly, he is not an extremist who will exhibit a feeling of superiority over people of other nations; he has also not been known for the overt advocacy of political independence for Nigeria, or of the Niger Delta from the rest of the country. I believe that Alagoa is a nationalist in the best sense of the word; he loves his country, not just at the national level but also at the local and even grassroots level; he is proud of that country and its achievements; he cares for it and for its positive development in the comity of nations. What he wishes for Nigeria at the national and international levels, he wishes for his own Niger Delta region and the Ijọ people in particular at the local level. That love he has been able to espouse and adumbrate in his devotion to the study of the people and the environment, which are closest to him, and he knows best.

Before a consideration of the various ways in which he has made this apparent, it is important to have some insight into his antecedents. What factors in his early life and upbringing have made possible the coalescence of nationalism and culture, which we see in him? It may help us to understand and appreciate what he has come to represent. He himself has admitted in his contribution to Dipo Ajayi's *This I Believe: The Philosophies and Personal Histories of 24 Nigerian Achievers, 2004* that it is *"not easy to define a personal philosophy of life in a manner sufficiently coherent and fully accessible to others"*. he has recommended that the best approach is to do it like a historian from the life story, the environments of family, community, school and work and from such information draw lessons. In his contribution to that volume he has given us a glimpse of his life history. The Niger Delta, where he grew up, he himself has described as a difficult environment; physical conditions are austere but support a rich, social and cultural life. His early life is one that provided him with the opportunity of being steeped in that culture and appreciating it. Indeed, he had no other option, but the impact on him was a positive one. The first nine to ten years of his life were spent with his maternal grandmother who was a herbalist and a priestess i.e. a practitioner of traditional medicine and a promoter of traditional religion. According to him, his grandmother prepared herbs for patients often without charging fees; she was also a repository of the folk tales, local histories and myths of his people and their gods. According to Alagoa, she also taught him that material goods are inferior to good works, a good name, a good heart and positive endowments.

It was only at the age of ten years that he came under the influence of his father in Nembe, and was exposed for the first time to what could be regarded as external influences in the appurtenances of Western civilization. He went to an Anglican primary school where he learnt to read and write in English and fortunately also in Nembe. He admitted that the translation of the Bible and hymns in Nembe by Pastor D.O. Ockiya of the Anglican mission provided inspiration as to the possibilities of creativity in the mother tongue, along with the dissemination of his cultural heritage in the international medium of English. For him, *"the teaching of local history provided a focus for commitment to the heritage"*. At home, his father, a polygamist provided another example of how to manage this cultural situation with a high degree of impartiality. He was also a public figure who sought no political office in the wider house system of Nembe city but constantly gave voluntary service in addition to assisting his less fortunate relations to meet their financial obligations to the colonial administration. In his own words: *"from my father I learnt to believe in the saving grace of education, an impartial discipline and in the character of responsible public service without hope or possibility of reward"*. What more ingredients of true and positive nationalism could be captured in that experience?

The awareness of his culture became more intensified when he gained admission to the prestigious Government College, Umuahia. The tradition of Government Colleges of his era was to emphasize the teaching of science and to encourage students to opt for science-based disciplines. But at Umuahia, he was taught by a history teacher who made the histories of Western European societies live and not too remote in their experiences from that of his own local community. Alagoa ended up as the only Art or Humanities student in his final year at Umuahia. It was not surprising that he opted to read History at the University of Ibadan. He came under the tutelage of

Professor K.O. Dike, the pioneer Nigerian historian who became his mentor and who, no doubt, was his hero. Alagoa in his paper, *Of Days, Bread and Mushrooms: The Historian as Hero*, in *Dike Remembered: African Reflections on History, Dike Memorial Lectures 1985-1995* (1998) which he edited, described Dike very significantly as a cultural nationalist. He stated that *"there is a cultural dimension to the building of national consciousness in which the historian can play a role"*. With the present seeming neglect of the teaching of history and its relevance in our national life, he states that *"it is the responsibility of historians, as men of culture and as members of the intellectual community to proclaim the truth that wisdom derives from the heritage of history, and that the experience of the ages embedded in culture is an essential ingredient of national development"*. Dike recommended Alagoa to study at the University of Wisconsin under Philip Curti; it was at Wisconsin that he also met and studied under Jan Vansina who demonstrated through his study and research of oral traditions the possibility of studying societies like those of Alagoa's Niger Delta where the conventional written sources on which professional Western-trained historians have relied for historical reconstruction are lacking or totally inadequate.

The story of Alagoa's encounter and escapades with oral traditions will be told in another contribution in this seminar and they need not detain us here. It is consequent reconstructions from such oral traditions and history that are most relevant for our discussion; they provide a significant dimension to our examination of Alagoa as a cultural nationalist. His antecedents have provided all the ingredients for the making of a cultural nationalist; the next issue that should be addressed is what he made of such rich endowment and grooming.

His professional life certainly reflects his commitment to the study of history and the significance of findings from history for the growth and development of the Nigerian nation. His Curriculum Vitae is replete with his publications in this regard. It will suffice to highlight a few of them as examples of his commitment. Of note here is *A History of the Niger Delta: An Interpretation of Ijọ Oral Tradition* published in 1972. According to him "*this study is an attempt to reconstruct the early history of the Ijọ people of the Niger Delta from their own traditions*". Such a work had not been done for any Nigerian group by the time he did. The book gives a fairly detailed account of the history of the Niger Delta people—covering the Niger Delta environment, the Western Delta fringe, the Central Delta, the Eastern Delta and the Northern Delta fringe. Earlier on in 1968 in his article on the *Ju Festival* among the Apoi Ijọ of Okitipupa, he had shown the extent of the spread of the Ijọ people and the survival of the basic elements of their culture even in a Yoruba environment. In *The Small Brave City State: A History of Nembe-Brass in the Niger Delta* (1964), he traces the history of the Nembe people from their origins, social and political organization, to their trading prowess; he describes their relationship with the British which culminated in the Akassa Raid of 1895 which resulted from the attempt of the British to deprive the people of their control of the hinterland trade. He discusses the effect on their culture of Christianity and other facets of Western civilization. This aspect of his contribution will be discussed below. There are in addition other papers dealing with Ijọ Origins and Migration, some of the traditional rulers of the Niger Delta such as Koko, Amanyanabo of Nembe, King Jaja of Opobo and Queen Kambasa of Bonny. There are also books and articles on other aspects of Nigerian and even African history.

The main thrust of his scholarship, however, has been on the Niger Delta. Such attention is significant and makes explicit the issues involved for a scholar from this area in the present Nigerian nation. The issue of marginalization of the Niger Delta and the feeling of its being neglected in the development of Nigeria has provoked discussion throughout the country. Indeed two publications by Onyoma Research Publications—*The Ijọ Nation in the New Millennium* (2000) and *The Uses of Hindsight as Foresight* (2004) to which I have had no access, might be useful in discussing this particular issue. Alagoa's contribution draws attention to the Niger Delta where these issues are very live. It builds an *esprit de corps* among the people based on the knowledge of their historical experiences. It brings forcibly to the attention of the rest of the nation the history, knowledge, experience and contributions of this fourth largest ethnic group. As he said in the article cited earlier, (*This I believe*) he believes that the commitment to the Nigerian nation can derive from strong attachments to specific environments. Such communities can provide evidence of tolerance of neighbouring and distant communities, which in practice develop relationships of mutual understanding and viable feelings of interdependence. It is also his belief that history can contribute to a fund of deep self-knowledge and understanding of neighbouring communities within the Nigerian nation.

It will be a great omission in this regard not to mention his contribution through his research findings to the debate on feminism and the participation of marginalized Nigerian women in the development of their country. In his articles—*Queen Kambasa of Bonny* (1992) and *God is Mother: A Historical Review of Women in the Development of Niger Delta Communities* (2003), he acknowledged women's contribution to the social, economic and even political life of this area in the past; the female principle is significant in Niger Delta religious thought, God being regarded as Mother and referred to in the feminine gender. The traditions of origin and development of the most prestigious artistic activities contained in them are accounts of women's creative contribution e.g. as in the EKINE or SEKIAPU society of the Kalabari. The history of Bonny and the emergence of Queen Kambasa as the ruler of that kingdom negates the idea that women cannot be rulers and be at the helm of affairs and decision-making; she was remembered as one of the most effective rulers in the domestic and foreign relations of that kingdom. Alagoa noted perhaps with some regret about our disappearing culture the fact that in present day Nigeria, it is not the law and tradition that are excluding women from governance but the will of men to keep them out. He provides through his accounts, strategies, which women can adopt to wield power. He concluded of Queen Kambasa that by strong-will combined with tact, she achieved much more than most men.

Alagoa's contribution, however, went beyond the interaction of Nigerians with Nigerians. He also had a clear-cut position on Nigeria's relationship with other nations and people, and he showed through his writings the need to maintain Nigeria's national integrity and protect our national culture. In his recent account of the Akassa Raid of 1895, *Beke You Mi: Nembe Against the British Empire* (2001), he concludes *"that the Nembe-British War of 1895 was a factor in the Nigerian history of the struggle against colonial conquest, as well as in the establishment of a Nigerian colonial system".* As for the impact of Christianity and Western civilizations he also had strong comments to make, based on the evidence of his historical research. He believes that Christian missionaries in Nembe destroyed the positive traditional values of the people, and by categorizing the people as pagans (heathens); and Christians imbued with Western ways, undermined the traditional unity that existed in Niger Delta communities. Unfortunately Western education also left the children between and betwixt two cultures, neither of which they can grasp effectively.

He also expresses great regret over the destruction and pilfering of our material culture. These objects he regards as a major repository of the cultural heritage of a non-literate people. In the symposium of *Nigerian Antiquities* in 1972, he, along with others, expressed unhappiness about the disappearance of Nigerian art objects particularly after the Nigerian Civil War. Apart from those destroyed by religious iconoclasts and those allowed to decay through lack of care, many were stolen and taken away overseas to be exhibited in foreign museums. He noted that several Niger Delta woodcarvings found their way to the CMS headquarters in London as samples of idols etc., British administrators carted some away and many are now to be found in museums in

Britain. He criticized the Antiquities Ordinance, which left many loopholes for despoilers of the Nigerian cultural heritage. He pointed out the fact that Nigerians are ignorant about the value of these objects and are therefore in need of education in this area. He made far-reaching recommendations for the protection of these objects and the promotion of our culture generally. It was at this symposium that we have one of the earliest pronouncements on the need for the establishment of a Ministry of Culture both at the state and federal levels as well as the building of museums to house and protect our antiquities.

Apart from his own research, which still continues, he was greatly involved in outreaches for the development of our culture. He was the prime mover of the Rivers State Research Scheme on which he served as Director from 1971 to 1977; it was a comprehensive multi-disciplinary study of the peoples of that state in the tradition of earlier research schemes in the country such as Benin, Yoruba, Northern and Eastern Research Schemes. Along with late Professor Kay Williamson and Professor Otonti Nduka, he also started the Primary School Readers in Local Languages so that pupils in their first few years in primary schools can speak their own language, and learn in English language and can read in both languages. The Onyoma Research NGO devoted to research and publications on the Niger Delta is his current brainchild. He was also the founding President of the Nigerian Association for Oral History and Traditions in 1989. It is not surprising that he became the President (1981-1983, 1991-1994) of the Historical

Society of Nigeria, one of the oldest professional associations in this country; he is a fellow of that society, and is currently the editor of its journal.

National recognition has therefore come to him in many areas where there is appreciation of his contribution to our culture and national development. He has been a member of the National Antiquities Commission, 1972-1976; Member, National Council of Arts and Culture, 1975-1976, 1990-1994; First Chairman, Rivers State Council for Arts and Culture, 1972-1975; Chairman, Rivers State Chieftaincy Review Commission, 1975-1976; Member of Nigerian Television Authority, 1984-1986; Member, Nigerian Copyright Council, 1989-1993; Member, National Merit Award Board, 1998-2001; and now, appropriately so, Pro-Chancellor, Niger Delta University, Wilberforce Island, Bayelsa State, 2001-2005. Of course, he is a Fellow of the Nigerian Academy of Letters, 2001 and a recipient of the Award of Excellence in History, Bayelsa State government, 2004.

The list is longer than I have enumerated; but Professor Alagoa deserves it all; he is a nationalist but of a special hue. He has not gone on the soap box to declare his manifesto; his scholarly and painstaking research proclaims him a nationalist from the roof tops, his findings lay open our culture and show the elements within it which can lead to the development of a strong, united nation which can do away with the fissiparous tendencies and which can enable it to hold up its head in the comity of nations. Alagoa has used his own cultural environment and knowledge as a springboard for raising issues of national interest and significance. He is only seventy-two (72) years of age; he is certainly not tired; all we can wish him is good health and strength as he continues to chart his path as a cultural nationalist.

8

Professor E.J. Alagoa: The Administrator

Abi A. Derefaka

Given Professor Ebiegberi Joe Alagoa's obvious erudition and his quiet and peaceful mien, only an awareness of his responsibilities in his early working life provide a clue that this meticulous and well informed scholar could be an effective administrator. Being a disciplined, cultured, and humane person, Professor Alagoa has been quite comfortable and effective in performing administrative roles during his impressive and meritorious career. Before he came into the University system, Professor Alagoa worked in the National Archives of Nigeria at Ibadan, Enugu, and Kaduna between 1959 and 1962 as Archivist/Senior Archivist.

He began his career in the University system as a Lecturer at the University of Lagos in 1965. Between 1966 and 1972, Professor Alagoa was a Senior Research Fellow at the Institute of African Studies, University of Ibadan. He became a Professor of History and Director, Centre for Cultural Studies, University of Lagos between 1972 and 1977. He was the first Dean, School of Humanities, University of Port Harcourt, 1977-1980. He was also the first Deputy Vice-Chancellor, University of Port Harcourt between 1980 and 1981. He was Acting Vice-Chancellor, University of Port Harcourt in 1982.

Thereafter, he was Dean, School of Graduate Studies twice. His first tenure was between 1985 and 1987. He was Chairman of the Niger Delta Research Group, Faculty of Humanities, between 1990 and 1998. However, to adequately appreciate the significance of his contributions as an administrator, it is necessary to look at the catalogue of his Public/Professional Service appointments.

He has been:
- Chairman, Rivers State readers project, 1967-present
- Director, Rivers State Research Scheme, 1977-1997
- Member, National Archives Committee, 1966-1970
- Member, National Antiquities Commission, 1972-1976
- Member, National Council for Arts and Culture, 1975-1976, 1990-1994
- First Chairman, Rivers State Council for Arts and Culture, 1972-1975
- Chairman, Rivers State Chieftaincy Review Commission, 1975
- Member, Council of the Rivers State College of Science and Technology, 1972-1975
- Member, Joint Admissions and Matriculation Board, 1978-1982
- President, Historical Society of Nigeria, 1981-1983, 1991-1994
- Member, Nigerian Television Authority, 1984
- Member, Nigerian Copyright Council, 1989-1993
- President, Nigerian Association for Oral History and Tradition, 1985-1994
- Member, Nigerian National Merit Award Board, 1998-2001
- Pro-Chancellor, Niger Delta University, Wilberforce Island, Bayelsa State, November 2001

- Chairman, Governing Board, Rev. D.O. Ockiya College of Theology & Management Sciences, Emeyal. Proprietor: Diocese of Niger Delta West, Church of Nigeria (Anglican Communion), 2004

Professor Alagoa's stint at the National Archives prepared him well for both his academic and administrative duties later in his career. Effective administration requires an understanding of communication techniques, especially how to write minutes to superiors and subordinates. It also requires familiarity with the conventional abbreviations used in minutes such as k.i.v., b.u., p.a., etc. It is also essential for an administrator to be familiar with the organogram of the unit, department, or establishment. A good administrator also identifies, deploys, and utilises human resources at his disposal adequately to achieve set goals within target time frames. He also maximises the utilisation of available material resources to ensure that the objectives of the establishment are met and staff welfare is not compromised. Put differently, a good administrator is an efficient manager of human and material resources to ensure that the objectives of the establishment are met and staff welfare is not compromised. Put differently, a good administrator is an efficient manager of human and material resources as well as time.

These criteria will be used to evaluate the performance of this colossus of our time in his administrative assignments. One should, however, indicate here that it is perhaps presumptuous of this writer to claim to be qualified to make judgmental pronouncements on the administrative competence and performance of his academic mentor. It is an assignment one was given to chronicle Professor Alagoa's contributions in the area of administration and that cannot be done without some evaluation of the significance of his contributions in this sphere.

At the National Archives, Professor E.J. Alagoa was a senior staff and was involved in administrative duties requiring reading of files and writing minutes as well as attending meetings. The management of documents in terms of documentation, cataloguing, storage, and retrieval were, however, his primary concerns. He learnt the ropes, as it were, of administration while working at the national archives. He also developed the ability to obtain, collate, organise, analyse, and utilise information which he had acquired during his undergraduate training in History at the University College, Ibadan. It is important to note that he also obtained a Certificate in Archives Administration from the American University, Washington DC in 1960. While at the National Archives he produced three archival monographs:

1. 1961. Series Inventory of the Records of the Provincial Office, Onitsha, 1896-1955. National Archives of Nigeria, Enugu Branch,
2. 1962. Special List of Records Related to Historical, Anthropological and Social Studies Among Provincial Administration Record Groups at the National Archives, Kaduna Branch.
3. 1962. Special List of Materials Concerned With Tribal and Related Studies Among Kaduna Secretariat Record Groups. National Archives, Kaduna Branch.

On his return from his studies at the University of Wisconsin, Madison, USA, where he obtained a Certificate in African

Studies in 1965 and a PhD in History in 1966, he was first a Lecturer at the University of Lagos and then a Senior Research Fellow at the Institute of African Studies, University of Ibadan between 1965 and 1972. He had to apply for and manage research grants, submit progress and final reports to granting authorities, and present research findings before his peers and seniors during this period. These involved adherence to administrative rules and procedures. Available records show that Dr E.J. Alagoa, as he then was, acquitted himself creditably in those tasks. Indeed in 1972 he had become a Professor of History. Although he was a member of the National Archives Committee between 1966 and 1970 and became Chairman, Rivers Readers Project from 1967, his appointments outside the University system requiring administrative duties began to increase from 1972. For example, he was the first Chairman, Rivers State Council for Arts and Culture and Member, Council of Rivers State College of Science and Technology between 1972 and 1975. He was also Member, National Antiquities Commission between 1972 and 1976. As the first Chairman of the Rivers State Council for Arts and Culture, Professor E.J. Alagoa laid down a very good foundation for the development of the Council. The administrative, professional and research structures established during his tenure have stood the test of time. During his tenure the Council was very active in drama productions, archaeological research and excavations, ethnographic research, museum development and publications. It was during his tenure that *Oduma* was published. It was also during his tenure that Ogoloma, Saikiripogu, Ke and Okochiri were excavated. Apart from

Oduma there were also other important publications sponsored by the Rivers State Council for Arts and Culture. One of these was Chief E.W.G. Opuogulaya's book on the Culture of the Wakirike (Okrika). Apart from encouraging such storehouses of indigenous knowledge like Chief Opuoguluya to commit their knowledge into writing, Professor E.J. Alagoa actively patronised and encouraged local fine and performing artists. It is also to Professor E.J. Alagoa's credit that he established an efficient and goal-oriented administrative system for the Rivers State Council for Arts and Culture. He has been a stickler for punctuality and regularity at work. He has also always had a keen interest in the maintenance of accurate and full records in all aspects of human and material resource management. The personal habits of making a list of activities for each day ahead of time, ticking each off as it is accomplished, and recording daily expenses incurred in detail, Professor Alagoa has brought to bear in his official administrative and research duties. These helpful habits which ensure proper time management, accountability, and transparency have been responsible for the meticulous and successful records he has left behind wherever his administrative skills have been required.

In the University system his first real administrative job was as Director, Centre for Cultural Studies, University of Lagos between 1972 and 1977. He set the Centre up as a multi-disciplinary Centre with famous Nigerian experts in music and musicology such as Professor Laz Ekwueme and others featuring prominently in the activities of the vibrant Cultural Centre. The legacy he left behind there both at the Department of History, where his academic assistance was utilised and at the Centre for Cultural Studies are an eloquent testimony to the success story of his career at the University of Lagos.

Meanwhile, toward the end of his formal employment at the University of Lagos, Professor E.J. Alagoa was involved in establishing a new University, which eventually became the University of Port Harcourt. He began his formal activities as an administrator at the University of Port Harcourt as the first Dean of the School of Humanities between 1977 and 1980. Between 1980 and 1981 he was the first Deputy Vice-Chancellor of the University, and in 1982 became Acting Vice-Chancellor of the University of Port Harcourt. Between 1975 when the University College of Port Harcourt was established as a College of the University of Lagos and when Professor E.J. Alagoa retired from the University of Port Harcourt, he was involved in the establishment and running of the Institution. This is why much of the insight one can gain of his administrative acumen in the University environment is to be searched for here.

The book, which Professor Theo Vincent, as Vice-Chancellor of the University of Port Harcourt commissioned Professor Alagoa to produce in July 1988, was to be, according to Professor Vincent, "a well researched and documented history" of the University. In his Introduction to the volume he says, "Indeed, an innovative spirit marked the very first meetings of the pioneer academic staff of the University on the 28th and 29th October, 1976 a year ahead of the first academic session" The first Vice-Chancellor (then Principal) Professor Donald E.U. Ekong, set the pattern in his opening address, to the effect that the new University would not routinely adopt the "academic and administrative practices, traditions or programmes" of older or more famous universities:

> Our approach here should be to determine our policies from first principles only, that is, first to identify our goals and our facilities for achieving them, and from there attempt to work out the best means of achieving them.

The meetings of October 28-29, 1976 laid down the principles and objectives which, it was hoped, would guide the orderly development of the University."

Before going into details of Professor E.J. Alagoa's contributions to the administration of the University of Port Harcourt, this writer would like to recall that Professor Alagoa played an active role in the search for where to site the University and one was privileged to have covered one of the meetings with the Rivers State Government officials and traditional rulers in 1975. As a young Administrative Officer I covered the meeting with the Secretary to then Military Government, Sir Francis Ellah, where the land for establishing the University was discussed. Perhaps at this point we should look at the recollections of a pioneer student of the University who is now a Senior Lecturer in the Department of English. This is to illustrate the meticulous planning that went into starting the new University off on a good footing. Eldred Green (1999: 77) says:

> Under the leadership of Professor Donald E.U. Ekong, its first Principal and later

Vice-Chancellor, for the institution adopted and maintained an attitude of friendliness to its host communities—immediate, Local Government, and State. Two instances properly illustrate this attitude. First was the fact that Professor Ekong went round Rivers State—reaching the more remote areas by helicopter—informing the people that at long last a University College had been approved for them and that academic activities would start in October 1977. The second was the commencement, early in 1977 of University Preparatory Classes (UPC) to prepare candidates for the Concessional Entrance Examination scheduled for about three months from then. Classes were held at the Port Harcourt Primary School and the Oromenike temporary campus of the Rivers State College of Education.

Professor E.J. Alagoa was clearly involved in fashioning out this approach. In the decision to be innovative, the School system (different from the Faculty system operational in the other Nigerian universities at the time) was adopted such that there were the Schools of Humanities, Social Sciences, Educational Studies but later the Institute of Health Sciences, management and Business Administration, and Engineering were added. Professor Alagoa (1999: 2) indicates how this innovation helped solve an important problem when he says, "The break of the sciences into three separate Schools ensured the achievement of the higher percentage of science against non-science student admission required by the

National Universities Commission, and which had proved difficult to achieve in many Nigerian universities." It would be interesting to find out if the change to the Faculty/Department system from the 1982/83 session still enables the University of Port Harcourt to satisfy the NUC requirement. However, it is important to note that the Senate meeting of march 25, 1977 codified the academic programme of the University into the guiding declaration known as the Statement of Academic Policies. By the appointment of the first Registrar of the University and establishment of requisite educational administrative units, the first Vice-Chancellor and his lieutenants ensured that there would be smooth administration in the institution.

Finally, one could look at the aims and objectives as set out in the law establishing the University of Port Harcourt and see to what extent the administrative structures and practices put in place by the pioneer staff were adequate for achieving those objectives. As Ejituwu (1999: 46) rightly points out, the objectives as set out in Decree 84 of September 20, 1979, which is the law establishing the University of Port Harcourt, are as follows:

(i) To encourage the advancement of learning and to hold all persons without distinction of race, creed, sex or political conviction the opportunity of acquiring a higher and liberal education.
(ii) To provide courses of instruction and other facilities for the pursuit of learning in all its branches, and to make those facilities available on proper terms to such persons as are equipped to benefit from them.

(iii) To encourage and promote scholarship and conduct research in all fields of learning and human endeavour.
(iv) To relate its activities to the social, cultural and economic needs of the people of Nigeria.
(v) To undertake any other activities appropriate for a university of the highest standard.

One can say that the policies, facilities, and procedures put in place at the School of Humanities where Professor Alagoa was the first Dean, and by the University of Port Harcourt where Professor Alagoa was the first Deputy Vice-Chanclelor laid solid foundation for incrementally working towards the realisation of the five objectives listed above. For example, the idea of Faculty courses from various Departments to be taken by all students of the Faculty is a carry over from the initial School system. Also the Community Service Courses which are University wide are, as Alagoa (1999: 5) explains:

> ... credit earning courses—devised in each discipline for one semester in the second and third years. Each course was intended to identify a practical problem in the communities around the University, and to address such a problem in order to work directly with the community to provide solutions derived from knowledge derived from the specific discipline. Students and staff were to be involved in the activities. The Community Service was the most direct challenge to the principle of knowledge for service to community, the inculcation of dignity of labour, and the practical application

of the motto, For Enlightenment and Self-Reliance.

Although Professor E.J. Alagoa is a team player, it is not difficult to see his hand in the choice of the University motto and crest which were derived from the mandate of the University as articulated by the pioneer staff of the University thus, "To contribute to national development, self-reliance, and unity through the advancement and propagation of knowledge, and to use such knowledge for service to the community and to humanity".

9

The X-Factor in the Life and Work of Professor E.J. Alagoa

Sereba Agiobu-Kemmer Pearse

Today the drums are rolled out, the drumbeat is loud and clear. From the heartland, Greetings and we salute Nembe.

Kala Ekulema Nembe

Kala Ekulema Nembe

Ama dọkọ dọkọ biokpọ.

We salute the womb that gave birth to another great and restless shark, a great son, Professor Ebiegberi Joe Alagoa, OON, FHSN, FNAL, Chief Kala Joe of Nembe Kingdom.

This brief presentation is not taken from the viewpoint of an academic treatise nor pretence to any extensive research, but is nonetheless meant to be a tribute to Professor E.J. Alagoa, his person, his character and his work i.e. his contribution the society at large.

One is doing so from an appreciation of the environment and socio-cultural influences, which defined the predilections of man, and processes of his occupation. In his work and collaborations, he is someone who has been gender sensitive and why? Then perhaps, to bring a lighter mood, to a very "Serebral" History Concourse. Having stated this objective, one will go a step further to explain the reason for the title of this paper: "The X-factor in the Life and Work of Professor E.J. Alagoa".

In the biological sciences, in the studies of sexual reproduction and genetics, we learn that when the cells lie side by side, having a pair of building blocks called chromosomes, the female pair consists of two X and the male, one X and one Y, i.e. XY. For the male to be born the Y must be present. For a female it must be X right through.

The principles of heredity also explain that the chromosomes consist of certain properties known as genes which also determine sex-linked character traits in individuals such as genetic disorders, what in the genes are called alleles. These factors are either X or Y packed. So you have the X or Y-chromosomes. From genetic links, the female genes are recessive when it comes to genetic disorders, while the male genes are expressive. In disorders, for instance, as colour blindness and haemophilia, the male gene is expressive. Women will be silent carriers; men are the ones who show these genetic disorders. The female will be a carrier instead for our vision.

This is a very rudimentary explanation of principles in biology from memory of secondary school days. Alright, pardon the elementary explanation, which is quite adequate, for the point to be made, that the title arose from borrowing the facts as presented in biology, known as the X-factor i.e. the female characteristics or femininity, is not confused with being effeminate, which is regarded as being weak in reference to a man.

Rather, femininity, is having a quality that is of a creative mind and acute senses, evidence of positive character traits, or attributes, that make one not only able to achieve certain goals, but also, to excel in the chosen fields of endeavour. The X-factor is a positive influence that has imparted special attributes to the subject, which has also directed his vision and reflected in all his work, even in the present preoccupation.

Let us look at the great impact, elements of the female gender, made on his life and works. It is not from a viewpoint of gender bias, but gender sensitivity. It is not a denial of the other Y-factor, the male gender's influence, nor of other influences from the natural, socio-cultural and academic environments, for instance.

Rather, it is an attempt to bring attention, to highlight, what oftentimes, we fail to acknowledg: the feminine perspective. This is done, either through ignorance, or just sheer neglect and omission.

Why this persists, one can only conclude that it is because, generally women's contributions and activities, are at best taken for granted, or not regarded as 'important'. To readdress this partial view, is the *raison d'etre* of this paper.

There is this popular adage that "the hand that rocks the cradle, rules the world". The hand that brings into the world, nurtures the new-born, in its first formative years, will be that of its mother, whether it's the biological or the many surrogate mothers, it will be a female hand within the family unit e.g. the wet-nurse and nannies in Western society. In Africa, where traditionally the society is polygamous, this is even more true, as children were usually not weaned before age 3 years or more, where mothers and other female members of the extended family, took care of the child. The first important human contact and relationship a child has and still does, is that bond with the 'mothers', members of the female gender.

The father at this stage is viewed in the far distance, not because he cares less, but because nature so dictates. By and large, an infant's need makes it to be more dependent on the mother. Childcare of the physical and emotional needs of the child, is one of the roles women play, defined as a maternal role by society. The importance of this maternal role and contribution to development is usually acknowledged in the reverse, more from the viewpoint of its negative consequences. We will come to that shortly.

One wants to draw out, first of all, the fact, that it is only logical, that the first emotional tie of a child, is to the female gender and its qualities, the X-factor. This is further buttressed by facts from developmental psychology which show clearly that the first few years of a human being are also its most important. They are the formative years for the moulding of the character and personality. The kind of physical and emotional stimuli to which the child is exposed to a very large extent, will determine its character and personality in adulthood.

One can begin to appreciate the importance of this maternal role and the magnitude of its responsibilities, as we also begin to appreciate the types of role-model, female factors, a child is exposed to, during the early formative years. Scientifically, it has been proven, to be the most critical time of its life. No wonder in our society, when one finds a deviant or badly behaved child, it is quickly referred to as 'the mother's child'. When the child is good or excels, it becomes the 'true child of its father'.

These statements contradict the facts of biological science, which link negative attributes to qualities in male genes. What then, one may ask, is the reason for such statements?

Far from being taken for granted, or overlooked, the feminine role and influence in the life of all of us, is too important to be thought, as of no consequence and not to be acknowledged.

Back to the point where we left off, that the appreciation of these feminine qualities, the X-factor, has to come, even if negatively and grudgingly. Some adages such as the Yoruba, say *"Iyani wura, omo ni jigi"*, "mother is a precious gold", and immediately on to add, "the child is the mirror". Why did the adage not stop at just extolling the virtue of 'motherhood' being golden? Is it just chauvinistic? And why is the child a mirror of the mother, even when it is a boy? One thinks it goes beyond the pale of the chauvinist darts, to one being reminded of the responsibilities of motherhood, i.e. maternal negligence and wrong influence.

The feminine attributes must be thought of to be good, otherwise a child will not be expected to be 'a reflection' of her, the X-factor. The female members of the family and the implication in the society, are seen as custodian of culture, tradition, morals and norms. Therefore, they also have, the responsibility of passing the right values, to the young ones, who are to be the next generation.

If a child is not properly brought up, knowing and imbibing the right values and expectations, it is taken for granted, that the foundation laying was wrong or faulty. The foundation builders are at the receiving end, where the blame is firmly thrown at them. Who else to blame, if not, they of the female gender, for failing to impart those fine feminine qualities—the X-factor!

Now that explains the contradictions of socio-cultural expectation, to the biological.

Again, one should point out, going by the same context, that the adage that gives all this acknowledgement to the feminine traits and influence, so succinctly, does so, giving praise to fatherhood the male, Y-factor. What adage there is only makes claims to the child that very well reflects, the attributes and influence of the X-factors, as a true-born child of its father and not a bastard, one to make the father proud. That child, is or can now be referred to as 'child of the husband', *"omo okoni o!"*.

For one to appreciate fully the life and work of Professor E.J. Alagoa is to understand the importance of the feminine influence. There is need to recognize the X-factor, to emphasize it more than any other. These attributes of femininity, at the same time are a reflection of the influence and contributions of members of the feminine gender, as shown in his approach and attitudes to life and work.

Professor E.J. Alagoa was born 70 years ago, to the royal Mingi lineage of Nembe. His father was Chief Joseph (Kalajoe) Ayibatonye Alagoa, his mother was Jane Kalajoe, née Obasi, of the royal lineage of Okpoama, paternally, while the maternal was of Ewoama.

We see at the very beginning of his life, how these promoters of the X-factor, took absolute charge of his early life and made lasting imprints on it.

As was the tradition of the time, the young mother Jane, travelled back home to her own mother in Ewoama to sojourn, to be looked after, until she delivered safely of her baby, before she returned back to Nembe. However, Jane left, leaving her young son E.J. with his grandmother, Madam Tuamain Mangite of Ewoama.

Okpoama, Ewoama and Nembe are in the Brass LGA. While 'E.J.' was dropped with Grandma, popularly called by everyone 'Ine' (mother or Granny) was to be propitious and defining to his life and career. This did not happen to his older brother, Maclean nor his younger, Solomon Iruo. However, a fact to note, was that his cousin, his maternal aunt Lokote's son, Benjamin Basuo, was also with grandmother Ine at the time.

Maybe it was felt, being of the same age, the playmates should not be separated.

The early formative years under the tutelage of Ine, was in the subject's own words 'the first role-model and life-long positive influence'. The coloration of her feminine attributes, must have been pervasive into all areas of the subject's life and his activities.

Ine was a herbalist, healer, griot and philanthropist, a humanist to the core. She exhibited a passion and commitment, not only to her profession, but also to socio-cultural and communal responsibilities. She was kind, caring, even-tempered, patient, sympathetic, sensitive to others needs. She was diligent and indefatigable in her work.

She was a woman of peace. She was also artistic and innovative, creatively making fabrics out of plantain and palm leaves and weaving baskets and fishnets.

Now, how many today, can combine all these skills, to be in multi-professional practice and successfully too? To be multi-disciplinary in approach, is to search in many directions, in order to achieve holistic value, the complete picture on the canvass, is made of various shades and segments that must be seen from various angles, and as a whole. Now, this multi-disciplinary approach was learnt early in life, from grandmother Ine. The acolyte has been faithful to all her feminine traits, like being "indefatigable, doing a thousand chores in one day".

Another very important and clearly inherited gene, from this promoter of the X-factor, is the role of the 'Griot', which is translated into the name Ebiegberi—the bringer of good news or the custodian of good news. He could recall that 'Ine' was 'a rallying point for the extended members of the family and local people, who gathered faithfully in the evenings, to listen to folktales, local history, myths, stories about ancestors and deities'.

Some revelations, that the course of a life-long career and vocation, had been imparted, so early, in the infant years, through this perfect role-model and 'guardian angel'. The fascination with stories, she told, histories she recounted and discussions she held with people, made lasting impression on a young character, so much so, as to make him become in later years, a national historian and international griot.

He is the national historian, who has applied western science to the study of the history of ethnic nationalities at home, while establishing in the international world fora, the authenticity of the history, from alternative perspectives, most especially that got from oral traditions, of his native land.

It was, a natural development and one, that was obtained from the name, Ebiegberi—the bringer or harbinger of the good news, through recollections and reflections of the past and present for a better tomorrow as in some of the works.

2004   *The Uses of Hindsight as Foresight: Reflections on Niger Delta and Nigerian History.*

1991   Antiquity and Future as Cultural Perspectives, *Culture and Decision Making in Nigeria.*

1981   *The Python's Eye: The Past in the Living Present*—1st Inaugural Lecture 1979, University of Port Harcourt.

All the pieces of work, can be said, to be a catalyst for reflection, on the past and present, in order, to proffer solutions and to predict a better direction to the future.

Under the influence of Ine Mangite, young 'E.J.' got imbued with her vision, mission, commission and example as a griot. A griot who is not only the custodian of the history and events, but also an interpreter, analyst forecaster. What a griot grew out, from under Ine's wing, to soar high, 'E.J.' One other quality to be noted, was how he must have been impressed, with the way and manner, she went about quietly, but resolutely doing her chores. No matter how many she had to perform in the course of a day, she stayed focused, to achieve the goal of serving humanity, through a combination of indigenous knowledge and applied technology, using whatever benefits accrued from the natural system, in an ecologically sustainable way, to bring solutions to the communal problems, be it health or economic, to add value, to both her environment and her community.

In her practice as a herbalist and care giver, one can conclude rightly, that she was operating a paradigm of integrated natural resources management, based even in those olden days on innovative strategies, critical technologies, even modern concepts of market economy and the ecology of sustainable human development, taking only that which was needed from the environment of the Niger Delta "might be a tough place in which to live and make a living", she demonstrated through "simple living, being dignified, independent minded and proud...that even though the conditions of life, could be spartan and austere, it also supported a rich social and cultural life, with enduring links to communities, economies and peoples of the Nigerian hinterland ... ."

What was learnt early, was how to achieve a goal. without wasting effort and words. It can be seen that all his writings possess brevity and clarity.

She was a moral and spiritual mentor, who imparted the value of a good name, above .gain and human relationship, above materialism. It was better to be an angel than a scoundrel. He, thought her to be truly an angel, how else, could one describe, someone, "who not only did not accept fees from her patients, but went further, to spend her own money and resources to cater for their needs". So do not think 'E.J.' gullible to all manner of 'sob stories', when you see him parting with money and other material goods liberally, to obvious fabrications of woe. It is not naively, but a sensibility to and compassion for the human condition. Compassion and generosity are inheritance of the X-factor, this acute love for humanity is in the genes. Always, the response, is to cry for help, that is beneath each sob story. The legacy of a good heart and spiritual endowments are being practically carried on.

Another attribute already mentioned, is that of the method of multi-disciplinary approach to proffering solutions, was given by Ine's example, which her acolyte, also manifests so well, in the methodology of his practice, as a historian, which can be attested to, by the many collaborators from various disciplines in the journey so far, and which is far from ending. There have been many collaborations with other historians from many fields and with the methodologies of other scientists and scholars, in other disciplines, such as archaeology, ethnography, anthropology, linguistics, languages, social science, art history, palaeontology, geography, and many more, in as much as they yield knowledge for the development of the history of the nation. This collaborations were done with individual scholars, or teams and institutions. This is typified in the trilogy publication on the Niger Delta Region as The Land People of Rivers, Bayelsa and Delta States, by Onyoma Research Publications.

Who was it, that taught him language, the beauty, the qualities, the values of the spoken word, as a means of expression, communications and as a tool for study? 'Ine' the first X-factor of course. His fascination and application of language, poetry and linguistics, produced results from very early:

1967   *Kien abibi onde fa pugu/Nembe (Ijọ) numerals.* Lagos.
1968   Songs as historical data for history: Examples from the Niger Delta. *Research Review* (Legon), **5**,1:1-16.
1986   *Noin nengia, bere nengia/More days more wisdom/Nembe proverbs.* Port Harcourt.
1987   [Editor] Oral historical traditions in Africa. *Tarikh* Vol. 8. Ikeja.

1990 *Tradition and oral history in Africa and the Diaspora: Theory and practice.* Proceedings of a symposium. Lagos.

1997 Proverbs as contested texts: The construction of a philosophy of history from African proverbs. *Embracing the Boabab Tree: The African Proverb in the 21st Century.* Edited by Willem Saayman. Pretoria.

1998 Amatemesuo kule [Drum praise poetry of community spirits]. *Comparative Literature and Foreign Languages in Africa Today.* Collection of Essays in Honour of Wilfred F. Feuser. Port Harcourt.

There are articles written in various journals such as:

1966 Oral traditions among the Ijọ of the Niger Delta.

1968 The use of oral literary data for history: Examples from the Niger Delta—proverbs

1971 Ijọ drumlore

1976 Dating Ijọ oral tradition

to cite some examples. The fascination with language and uses of the spoken word, is one that is enduring. One can recall even the many collaborations with a promoter of the X-factor, Professor Kay Williamson, such as the 'primers', for the "The Rivers Readers Project" development of minority languages.

1981 Ancestral voices: Oral historical texts from Nembe, Niger Delta

The griot faithfully retells the stories of great legends and national events, so we have all along, from the beginning of the career, that started professionally, in the early 60s and spanning up to the 90s, stories of the exploits of national heroes and heroines and of the nations, side by side.

Examples are many:
1960   Akassa Raid 1895
1964   The small brave city-state: A history of Nembe (Brass) in the Niger Delta.
1970   Jaja o Opobo: The slave who became king.
1972   [With Fombo] A chronicle of Grand Bonny.
1975   King Boy of Brass
1978   [With Kay Williamson and Ezekiel Gbobate] Kingfisher and the woman. *Kiabara* Vol. 2, 35-54.
1980   King William Koko of Nembe.
1986   Sagbe Obasi: Amanyanabo of Okpoama 1845-1862
1989   Contributions in *Great Historians from Antiquity to 1800: An International Dictionary*, edited by Lucian Boia (New York)
1992   Queen Kambasa of Bonny. *Nigerian Women in Historical Perspective,* edited by Bolanle Awe.
1995   People of the fish and eagle: A history of Okpoama in the Eastern Niger Delta.
2001   *Beke You mi: Nembe against the British Empire.*

However, this is a Griot with a different perspective, a Griot in the new millennium practising an age-old vocation with modern day tools of science and hi-tech.

The subject had been imbued with an appreciation of cultural mores, civics and the artistic expressions right from infancy, even in the small community of Ewoama, which is a microcosm of Nembe's spiritual and cultural heritage. Culture and artistic (all creative) means of human expression, the studies of its various disciplines and processes, in the making of human interactions and events, are necessary parts of the composite work and preoccupation of this historian's life. There is an intermingling of the aesthete, humanist, patriot, social reformer, and leader.

The X-factor produces sensitivity, or keenness to artistic expression, in the acquiring of and appreciation of various craft skills and in the arts of performance and production; like storytelling, singing, dancing, masquerading and festivals, that he became a lover of the arts and consequently a patron and promoter. This is an attribute of creative femininity, the contribution from his grandmother Ine and other women in the extended family, but first and foremost from his grandmother. The reinforcement of the X-factor army continues unabated in their daily conversations, songs and attendance to all socio-cultural issues.

Evidence can be found in his work pertaining to the study of culture as an art life, its products as instruments of development. Examples:

1964 Idu: A creator festival at Okpoama (Brass) in the Niger Delta.

1971 Antiquities in the Niger Delta and the Rivers State. Edited by E.J. Alagoa and Bolanle Awe.

1973 Brass, Bronze sculpture, Calabar, Cassava (Africa), Drumming, ritual and code language, Ibo people, Culture, States, Maize, introduction and production in all Africa, Nok culture, early iron age, West Africa, Sculpture, all African in *Dictionary of World History*, edited by G.M.D. Howat and A.J.P. Taylor.

1982 Owuaya: Mother of masquerades. In *The Masquerade in Nigerian History and Culture,* edited by N. Nzewunwa.

1983 Present-day cultural heritage. In *The Use of Cultural Heritage in Nigerian Education*, edited by Pai Obanya and Emma Arinze.

1985 Nineteenth century political culture in the Eastern States of Nigeria. In *Evolution of Political Culture in Nigeria*, edited by J.F. Ade Ajayi and Bashir Ikara.

2000 Museums and history in the Niger Delta. In *Museums and History in West Africa*, edited by Claude Daniel Ardouin and Emmanuel Arinze.

The many aunts, both maternal and paternal and in-laws, (his wife's own aunts), are all members of the household, nuclear and extended. They have been able to create the strong maternal environment to exude a pervading aura of femininity, a close-knit tapestry firmly held in place, by an enterprising, industrious and supportive wife, Lady Mercy G. Alagoa.

At this juncture, it is pertinent to point out, the fact also, that the Nembe culture, is to some extent matrilineal, especially in matters of inheritance. Unlike, what generally obtains elsewhere, in Nembe, for instance, a man's nephew, by full-blooded sisters, can inherit property from him, but not chieftaincy title or kingship, which must come by male line. But then, the poser how did King Boy Amain, nephew of Mingi, become so powerful to become Amanyanabo, Mingi (1830-1846)?

The mother must have been the Mingi's sister with very strong X-factor with which she imbued her son.

The Alagoas are descendants of King Boy Amain. The picture becomes clearer, if we find that the same attribute, the X-factor persists in the present. There is and always had been, a strong force of women, surrounding the subject, to protect, to create, a calm peaceful atmosphere, for industrious and meaningful pursuits to thrive.

In Nembe Ijọ worldview, the Creator—God, is given feminine attributes, which makes the possessor of the X-factor, to be imbued with godliness and creativeness. No wonder, one of Professor E.J. Alagoa's studies is "God is Mother", a contribution in *Women In Nigerian History: The Rivers and Bayelsa States Experience*', edited by N.C. Ejituwu and A.O.I. Gabriel for Onyoma Research Publications.

Nembe men and women, are quiet, dignified, unruffled by the storms and vicissitudes of life. They are hospitable, but if pushed to the wall, they turn to face their opponent squarely and will not relent until they draw blood. The appellation of 'Restless Shark' suit their psyche.

The strength of character, diligence, resourcefulness and industry, are attributes of creative femininity, well demonstrated in the lives of all the women (and men) who have contributed to moulding our subject's life, character and work.

This is best epitomized by the present matriarch of the family, Mrs Elsie Egein (née Aga) his youngest maternal aunt, a ninety plus years old lady, with about 10 children, over 40 grand children, and about 50 great grand children, who still goes farming and fishing. So are all the women in the family: good, reliable in character, indefatigable and industrious. The X-factor is very restless in spirit and active as a soul. To be so active at an age many would have retired, is eloquent testimony to inherited X-factor in the subject's lineage. Any wonder, he is more active in retirement now, more than ever? It is a fine trait, the indefatigable spirit in Professor E.J. Alagoa.

Before one is accused of total gender bias, though one is merely making a reversal of the usual trend. At this time, let us dwell, on a legacy from both the female as well as the male gender. This is to be found in the subjects preoccupation with social and current affairs and issues of development. As he admits to what he terms, 'a public leadership role,' in performing civic duties, to also be a conflict resolutionist, was inherited from the grandmother who sought no status, for her position, nor did the father, look for political office, or reward, while performing and contributing to public office. The concern was for the common good of the community and national development.

This is very true of our subject E.J. Alagoa, Chief Kalajoe of Nembe, Eminent Professor of History, Pro-Chancellor, Niger

Delta University; Officer of the Order of the Niger (OON), Fellow of the Nigerian Academy of Letters (FNAL) 2001, Fellow of the Historical Society of Nigeria (FHSN) 1982, Justice of the Peace, Bayelsa State 1999, Knight of St. Christopher (KSC), Niger Delta West Diocese, Church of Nigeria Anglican Communion 2001.

The concern for on-going socio-political processes and current affairs is not that of a power and status seeker, his interest and concern is manifest in his work' (especially post 90s to the present) making him an analytical commentator, one in the practice of politics of development and service to humanity, rather than of wealth and self aggrandisement.

His public stand or role of community leader, critical commentator and ombudsman is carried out quietly, in humility, but with a dignified and resolute stance; making lucid and clear arguments, that also proffer solutions, in every public presentation he makes.

Professor E.J. Alagoa

We acknowledge today the great contribution and giant strides you have made and continue to make along with numerous colleagues and collaborators, in time and space.

There were members of the other kind, along the way, of course, more acknowledged and given due recognition, but not so the X-factor in the life and work of Professor E.J. Alagoa.

However, today we blow open the lid to reveal the other secret, that also the intellectual brilliance and personality per excellence are in the bloodline, in the genes, in the X-factor!

The drum beats continue, almost deafening, and will be even louder for a long time to come.

Kala Ekulema Nembe

'Kala Ekulema Nembe

Ama ḍọkọ ḍọkọ ḅiokpọ.

10

Professor E.J. Alagoa As An Intellectual Leader

Atei Mark Okorobia
and
Kingdom Eke Orji

I. **Introduction**

We think Professor Chinua Achebe was right when he asserted that one of the greatest problems confronting contemporary Nigeria is that of leadership. And it is doubtful if any critic can successfully contradict him, if he or she would make an objective and dispassionate reconnaissance of the natural and human environments of the country. This, perhaps, informs the recent upsurge in the interest of many writers in the biography and auto-biography of men and women in leadership positions in different departments of life.

While some of these efforts are well researched and are enlightening, inspiring and helpful to historians, in their desire to illuminate the past and the present, many are at best, borne out of less than altruistic motives. They tend to serve more as works of self-justification and as propaganda stuff. In our present effort, the goal is apparently not to create a drum and trumpet biography of Professor Alagoa. We aim simply to make a scholarly attempt at distilling and explicating the roots and manifestations of the universally celebrated leadership qualities and laurels of the sage, to serve among other purposes, as an instrument for inspiring the present and future generations of Nigerians generally, and scholars in particular.

II. A Theoretical Perspective

To establish an objective basis for our discussion on Alagoa as an intellectual leader, we consider it important to clarify some key concepts to be engaged in the discourse, namely an 'intellectual' and a 'leader'. Who is an intellectual, and what are his commitments? And who is a leader and what are the qualities of a good and effective leader? It is after we have answered these preliminary questions that we can easily answer the more fundamental questions of whether or not Alagoa was and is an effective intellectual leader. If he was/is, then, we may also proceed therefrom, to assess the lessons that can be distilled and learned from his example of leadership.

(a) Who is an Intellectual? What are His Commitments?

In the context of our present concern, we may simply see an intellectual as a person who searches and possesses knowledge, and attempts to employ such knowledge to explain the problems of society with a view to finding solutions to them (Okoye 1980: 68). In other words, an intellectual is a man or woman who produces ideas, ideas about just any issue, and spreads same to others. Thus throughout history, we find that intellectuals are generally known to be persons who strive to discover the truth, propagate the truth, defend the truth, and in some cases, even die for the truth.

In terms of commitment, therefore, the intellectual is essentially a social critic, a person whose concern is to identify, to analyse, and in this way to help overcome the obstacles to a rational social order. As such he or she becomes the conscience of the society and a spokesman. The intellectual is therefore seen as a trouble maker and a nuisance by the establishment, which, for the most part, is concerned with preserving the status quo. Similarly, the intellectuals in the service of the establishment also see intellectuals outside as being either utopian, metaphysical, or even subversive, if not seditious.

We note that throughout history, the lives of great thinkers, whose consistent and persistent dedication to the elemental values of truth, love, beauty, peace and progress have given a new dimension to the life of the society, and have constituted important watersheds in the evolution of nations. To remain a conformist after discovering the truth of the deficiencies of any aspect of life would therefore portray an intellectual a coward and failure. For, as a rule, the future a society dreams of does not come about by itself. It results from the quality of deliberate choices made in the present. It is the responsibility of the intellectuals to provide leadership to the masses for the creation of the needed social transformation. The importance of this cannot be over-emphasised. The widespread ignorance and penury of the ordinary people in our part of the world, against the backdrop of their great thirst for sustainable development must be seen both as a challenge and as an opportunity by the intellectuals to work for better models of society for their people.

Before suspending further discussion on who the intellectual is, and what his commitment are should be, it is necessary to note that unlike other parts of the world, in Nigeria, the middle class intellectuals who are expected to guide the much talked about change, have historically lacked a strong economic base. This has easily forced them to be opportunists dependent on groups that have, through generally unwholesome means, captured political and financial powers. The unfortunate consequence of this is that the average Nigerian intellectual, professional, academic or political bureaucrat, is ever adjusting his values to prevailing orthodoxies, forever denying his ideals of yesteryear, instead of censuring those of today as if being consistent will betray his 'little mind' (Okoye 1980: 72).

(b)   Who is a Leader? Who is an Intellectual Leader?

A leader is one who guides by influence, or one who directs, by going before or along with the led. For one to be a leader, then, he or she must have followers, otherwise he or she ceases to be a leader. A leader is a person who dares to be himself and is able to express him or herself fully. Leaders are therefore persons who 'know who they are, what their strengths and weaknesses are, and how to fully deploy their strengths and compensate for their weaknesses' (Monroe,

1993: 19). Leaders are persons who know what they want, why they want it and how to communicate what they want to others. In another sense, a leader may also be seen as that person invested with authority by the common weal, or who plays the role of guardian in the proper ordering of the life of a people. Generally speaking, leadership has to do with one's ability to inspire others to become and fulfil themselves through example. Going by Monroe's analysis, this must include one's capacity to influence, inspire, rally, direct, encourage, motivate, induce, move, mobilize and activate others 'to pursue a common goal or purpose while maintaining commitment, momentum, confidence and courage' (Monroe, 1993: 30).

This leads us to the related question of what constitutes the ingredients of good or effective leadership. Experts in leadership studies have identified the following qualities and characteristics as the hallmarks of effective leadership:

1. He/she must possess a clear sense of purpose, that is, knowing why he or she exists.
2. He or she must be able to develop strong passion for fulfilling his or her identified purpose in life.
3. He or she must possess a high level of integrity, to be truthful to him or herself by knowing his or her strength and weakness, and deliberately strive for perfection while accepting criticism in good faith.
4. He or she must work hard to earn the trust of co-labourers and followers.
5. He or she must be curious, daring and adventurous by his or her willingness to face challenges, to oppose

unproductive traditions, to experiment novel ideas. He or she must not be discouraged by occasional setbacks, but must see such as the raw materials for future successes.

6. He or she must be ready to sacrifice his or her comfort, personal interest, and even his or her life in the course of serving the identified purpose.

From the foregoing, we may say that an intellectual leader is one, who through conscious efforts, has been able to discover the truth in a particular field or fields, and succeeded to a large extent, in propagating, directing, inspiring, motivating and influencing man and society with that truth.

Having clarified the key concepts to be employed in the discussion, we now return to the major concern of this paper—the extent to which Alagoa can be seen as an intellectual and as a leader.

III. Alagoa as an Intellectual Leader: The building Blocks

If we accept the theory that every person is a product of nature and nurture, his or her bio-physical and socio-cultural milieux, then it would be easy to appreciate the position we are proposing that Alagoa as an intellectual leader was the inevitable fruit of the complex interplay of the influences of the much celebrated inclement deltaic ecology of his nativity, and his reflected pride in the great exploits of his brave and rich ancestry, especially in the heyday of the trans-Atlantic trade between European supercargoes and legendary merchant princes of the Niger Delta city-states.

Specifically, the following factors and persons are the most outstanding among the key sources of influence that translated Ebiegberi, the otherwise 'village folk' from the creeks and mangrove swamps of the Niger Delta into the intellectual giant and meteor, and Emeritus Professor of History that is today respected by both friends and foes alike, universally.

First, is his grandmother. Professor Alagoa has himself been very forthcoming at every opportunity that provides itself to acknowledge the early and powerful influence his maternal grandmother, Madam Tuamain Mangite of Ewoama, an offshoot settlement of Okpoama, exercised on him. According to Alagoa, even though his grandmother was a workaholic,

> At evening time, local people and her extended family, to which she provided rallying point, gathered at her house front to listen to folk tales, local history, myths and stories of the gods (Alagoa, 2004: 63)

Without much elaboration, it is easy to see how the tender and impressionistic mind of Ebiegberi would have been arrested by these regular folk tales, local history, myths and stories of the gods.

Second is the nature of the teachers that taught him and the schools he attended. As a pupil. Alagoa was, in addition to the English language, also taught to be literate in the Nembe-Ijọ dialect. Equally important here, is the fact that this was happening at a time when the Anglican Mission was creating an enabling environment for literacy in the local language to prosper. It was this environment that had pushed up the Nembe literary gurus, such as the Reverend Daniel Ogiriki Ockiya. The translation of the Holy Scriptures, hymns and liturgy into Nembe- Ijọ by Rev. Ockiya provided such an influence that no serious minded young person could escape the infectious inspiration to what Alagoa himself refers to as

> 'the possibilities of creativity in the mother tongue along with dissemination of the cultural heritage in the international medium of English' (Alagoa, 2004).

Again, the missionary education Alagoa received continued to place great premium on the teaching of local history, which we saw earlier, he has been initiated into in his pre-school years by his grandmother. Similarly, the emphasis on reading and writing skills compelled the learner to pay more attention to the sharpening of his or her intellectual potentials. This trend was given an added boost when Alagoa became a student of the prestigious Government College, Umuahia from 1948 to 1953. The College taught its students to read widely and excel, though in the sciences, mainly. At the University College, Ibadan where Alagoa graduated into from Umuahia, he was turned into a confident graduate by the likes of Professor K.O. Dike, but had also been given the kind of orientation and training that would guarantee him a place in the sun of professional practice in history, anywhere on earth. But, perhaps, more than anyone else, Alagoa had been influenced intellectually by Professor Jan Vansina at the University of Wisconsin. Alagoa himself came close to confirming this when he said:

> 'In Jan (Vansina), I found my convictions in the essential validity and possibilities of oral tradition confirmed, and provided with the techniques for realizing my own agenda" (Alagoa, 2004)

Others who had also contributed to making an intellectual leader out of Alagoa were Professors Dike and Jacob Ade Ajayi. According to Alagoa, Professor Ade-Ajayi provided for him a 'model'.

Finally, Alagoa has also been moulded by psychological and sociological factors into becoming the intellectual hero he is today. The psychological factors include the fact of his beginning formal education at the late age of ten. Alagoa felt uncomfortable about this and for a long time, he lived under a sense of being behind members of his biological age group in education, and therefore had an inherent compulsion to cover more distance in a shorter space of time than his peers, at school. The aggregate consequence of this self-imposed psychological burden was the speed with which he rose through the intellectual ladder—he became a Professor at the age of 39, only 7 years after being involved in academics as a lecturer. Indeed Alagoa has spent greater part of his eventful life as a Professor than as a Doctor, or other such categories. This is what we may refer to as the Alagoa paradox: the last becoming the first among his peers.

The sociological influences on him were the stable family life he has always enjoyed: peer pressures; as well as the comments and criticisms of his fellow intellectuals and students.

IV. Alagoa's Intellectual Leadership Efforts

Alagoa's intellectual contributions have established him to be a leading figure in two distinct, though related aspects of historical scholarship. One is methodological, while the other is regional (Ejituwu, 1997: iii)

In the area of historical methodology, Alagoa's most enduring contribution is in the promotion of oral historiography as an acceptable tool of historical research. In emphasizing the potential of oral data, Alagoa has not in any way turned blind eye on the pitfalls associated with them. Not at all. Rather, he has counselled consistently, on the need for historians employing oral data to supplement the oral with other sources, particularly, archaeological, ethnographic, linguistic and palynological sources, as well as the other human and social science disciplines.

To give practical meaning to this effort, he has done more than anyone else, to recruit scholars of various backgrounds and persuasions into an interdisciplinary methodology? It was in his attempt at choosing an appropriate place to experiment this methodology that Alagoa broke into his second area of his contribution, regional history. And his choice was the Niger Delta region wherein both Professor K.O. Dike, Dr G.I. Jones and Professor Robin Horton and Professor Kay Williamson have worked.

Alagoa's first result from his effort was his successful establishment and sourcing of fund in 1971 for what was named Rivers Research Scheme. It was domiciled initially at the Institute of African Studies at the University of Ibadan. Though he left Ibadan for the University of Lagos not long after the commencement of the Scheme, there is evidence that he continued to lead or sponsor many fruitful archaeological (and sometimes palynological) studies, under its auspices, to different sub-regions of the Niger Delta.

Alagoa's effort received further boost following his ultimate movement from the University of Lagos to the University of Port Harcourt, nearer the heart of the Niger Delta. Horton (1997: 196) has aptly captured this significant breakthrough by Alagoa:

> 'Once settled, he lost no time in persuading other Niger Delta specialists to follow him. Over the years, his persuasive powers in this respect, have resulted in a unique concentration of such specialists. The concentration includes historians, archaeologists, anthropologists, comparative religionists and linguists.'

Within the University of Port Harcourt, this concentration has started reproducing itself. Many of the students were encouraged to do their research seminars, projects and theses and dissertations on the land and people of the Niger Delta. Externally, this had greatly enhanced the rating of the University among national and international researchers as the centre of excellence for Niger Delta Studies.

We need not over-emphasize the fact that Alagoa's intellectual leadership efforts have not been limited to providing direction, inspiration and motivation to scholars alone. He had, and has been active in providing equally inspiring and motivating leadership to participants in other sectors of the economy, polity and society. We can mention a sample of such efforts.

First, we wish to recall that since 1967 when he was still at Ibadan, Professor Alagoa has been organizing men and women across the Central and Eastern Niger Delta under the auspices of the Rivers State Readers Project to develop languages of the region. Here, he had enjoyed the very strong cooperation of the late Professor Kay Williamson, a linguist.

Between 1966 and 1970, he was equally active as a member of the National Archives Committee, while from 1972 to 1976, he was a member of the National Antiquities Commission. His days as pioneer Chairman of the Rivers State Council for Arts and Culture from 1972 to 1975 was perhaps the golden years of that Council. In addition to the usual singing and dancing, generally emphasized by such institutions, he endeavoured to create a council that encouraged and promoted holistic development of all facets of the people's history, culture and the arts, including a strong tradition of intellectual development. He has been elected President of the pioneer intellectual society in Nigeria, the Historical Society of Nigeria twice, from 1981 to 1983 and from 1991 to 1994. As the leader of this group, he provided new vision and inspiration to members and moved the Society to higher grounds, making them to honour him with the prestigious fellowship, Fellow of the Historical Society of Nigeria (FHSN) in 1982.

It is instructive to note that a veritable leader must be selfless. Professor Alagoa is ever willing to lend a helping hand to his students and colleagues. We have heard of intellectuals who are very reluctant to part with their books to any researcher. Some even ask for collaterals before they could 'loan' their books to any researcher. A genuine leader identifies with the plight of the led and Professor Alagoa demonstrates this virtue in his encounter with whoever seeks his generous and amiable assistance.

A leader as a visionary knows that he will retire some day, and as such would need successors. Therefore, Professor Alagoa spends ample time breeding successors in the different sub-fields of history. Hardly would you meet Alagoa on his return from a conference, workshop, study or sabbatical leave that he did not share his experiences with his colleagues. Through this means he has built and continues to build a very strong crop of successors in archaeology, history and cultural studies.

Though retired from active service, this intellectual colossus is not tired. There is every indication that in retirement, Professor Alagoa has become, even more productive as an intellectual leader. Operating from his new base at the Onyoma Research Centre in Port Harcourt, he has been mobilising intellectuals in various fields to continue the study of the land and people of the Niger Delta, paying particular attention to the history, culture, environment and developmental problems of the region. He has himself, also been more active in areas of community service that need the application of historical knowledge and his many years of experience, working and living in the Niger Delta. His latest publication, *The Uses of Hindsight as Foresight: reflections on Niger Delta and Nigerian History* is a compendium of some of the problem-oriented papers presented at various fora. Currently, he is also Chairman of the Ijọ History Project, the aim of which is to produce a scholarly study and document the contributions of the Ijọ at home and in the Diaspora.

V.   **Conclusion**

As scholar, Professor Alagoa has established himself almost as an institution in the area of African historiography. His originality in the use of the oral tradition in interpreting African history has endeared him to peers at home and abroad. Scholars from Europe and America frequently come here to consult him in various aspects of their research topics. A true believer in the practice of inter-disciplinary methodology, he is open to new ideas, new materials and new values. It is not surprising that he is pre-eminently tolerant in his approach to issues. He is innovative without being abrasive. Keen on intellectual leadership, he has used his position to enhance research and scholarship.

We cannot enumerate here the various assignments given him by the Rivers and Bayelsa States as well as the Federal governments, in recognition of his ability to contribute positively to the cultural life of the nation. They simply attest to his intellectual and morel integrity as a scholar and intellectual leader.

It should be clear from the foregoing that Professor Alagoa's research and leadership abilities are established beyond doubt, and that he more than deserves the honour accorded him. It was based on these and more that at its 302nd meeting held on Wednesday, May 25, 2005, the Senate of the University of Port Harcourt deliberated on a recommendation by the Faculty of Humanities and the History and Diplomatic Studies Department on Alagoa's impeccable records as an intellectual leader, and approved his appointment as Emeritus Professor of History of the University of Port Harcourt, with effect from 25 May 2005.

11

The Essence of E.J. Alagoa

Adiele E. Afigbo

1. A life of intense commitment to his profession and to his field of interest i.e. to his people; of commitment to his people through commitment to his profession and commitment to his profession through commitment to his people. A demonstration in our profession (History) and times of the time-honoured truth that the general and the universal are also embodied in the singular and the particular.

2. A life of sober, sedate, serene and eirenic scholarship. Not for him that view in which scholarship is a form of warfare in which you neither give nor ask for quarter.

3. A life that is an epitome of that far of and elusive goal of *Afrikanistik* scholarship—that is inter-disciplinary co-operation and approach. Of all our historians he is the most happily at home with what the ethnographers, the anthropologists, the archaeologists, the linguists, the palynologists etc. are saying or doing. Above all he has worked productively with most of them to advance historical scholarship generally and Ijọ (Izọn) history in particular. Thus we are talking of a life of intensive

and perceptive exploitation of the historians' sources—written, oral and others.

4. A life of quiet revolution in theorizing on the history of the Blackman in general and of the Niger Delta in particular. Dike used the Niger Delta to revolutionize African history by showing that the Blackman is human and rational. E.J. Alagoa has used the Niger Delta to show that the Blackman was not lying in limbo waiting for the providential advent of the white man to stir him into socio-political evolution. As the Abakaliki Igbo say "we were weaving cloth before the Aro came with European textiles". The Delta peoples, and for that matter the Africans, Alagoa has shown, were already engaged in local, regional and international trade as well as in the organization and running of state systems before the white man came in the 15th century. He has also revised our knowledge of Ijọ origins. The Ijọ are not just an amalgam of Edo, Igbo and Ibibio fragments as earlier proposed. They are an ancient people with a linguistic identity going back some 5000 years.

5. A life that can be described as the most successful, the most productive and the most glorious of those that have committed themselves to the study of the Niger Delta from very early days. In ranking, Alagoa stands as number 1 amongst all the humane and social scientists who have given their life to the study of the Niger Delta from the days of the Portuguese and Dutch slave captains on.

6. A life of dedication to capacity building in the intellectual profession and to community service.

7. Finally, a life that emphatically reminds us of the sovereignty of soul over the body. Otherwise how do we explain the frail-looking *corpus* which we see and touch and address as E.J. has been able, for these many decades, to arrive "again and again at the market with fresh vegetables" as the immortal and irrepressible J.P. Clark (as he then was) put it in defining a good driver in his collection of poems *The Victims?*

SUPPLEMENT

HISTORY MEETS JAJA OF OPOBO

1

Address Presented to His Royal Majesty The Amanyanabo of Opobo, King Dandeson Jaja by The Chairman, Organising Committee of The History Concourse to Celebrate the Life and Work of Professor Ebiegberi Joe Alagoa, Pro-Chancellor, Niger Delta University, Sunday, May 1, 2005

Abi A. Derefaka

Your Majesty:

On behalf of the Organizing Committee of the History Concourse to mark the retirement from active service of an illustrious son of the Niger Delta, who has devoted his life to the study of the Land and People of the Niger Delta, Professor E.J. Alagoa, I wish to thank you for graciously granting the participants at this Concourse audience today. His family, especially Lady M.G. Alagoa, would also wish to thank you for being part of this celebration. Your ascendance to the exalted throne of your famous ancestor, which brought to an end the over twenty years of tussle for the throne, forebodes progress, prosperity and unity for your ancient kingdom. Permit me to observe that the entire people of the Niger Delta and indeed Nigeria, need to learn the lesson from you and your subjects about how you managed a crisis that had the potential of tearing your kingdom apart with such civility and adherence to the rule of law.

The History Concourse to honour Professor Alagoa began yesterday with the opening of an exhibition of the works of three fine artists, who are sons of the Niger Delta at the Orogbum Crescent residence of this erudite academic and astute administrator. This was followed immediately by a rich harvest of the reflections of his close academic associates on various aspects of the life and work of Professor E.J. Alagoa at a three-session seminar that lasted till about 5 p.m.

Those who participated in the Seminars include Dr Gabriel Okara, Professor Abdulahi Mahdi, Vice-Chancellor of Gombe State University and eminent Historian; Professor Okon Edet Uya, another eminent Historian and former Ambassador; Professor Bolanle Awe, Pro-Chancellor, University of Nigeria, Nsukka; Professor Adiele Afigbo; and Professor Nkparom C. Ejituwu among other notable academics. The folder for the Concourse speaks for itself. In the evening a cultural night was organized in honour of this icon of Niger Delta Studies. Indeed it is extremely appropriate that this important event is climaxed by a visit to your Majesty and the ancient kingdom of Opobo.

It is with great pride in professor Alagoa's contributions to the study of the peoples and cultures of the Niger Delta that the Organising Committee and the eminent Scholars in this entourage present this token of our appreciation, consisting of the publications of Onyoma Research Publications founded by

Professor E.J. Alagoa, for your Palace Library. Once again we thank you for making it possible for this distinguished group to accompany Professor E.J. Alagoa to come to Opobo and congratulate you in person on your coronation as the Amanyanabo of Opobo. Finally, it is important to note that Professor Alagoa was appointed member of the Board of the Jaja Foundation in 2001 although its activities are yet to take off. In a sense, therefore, we have brought you one of your own in yet another hour of glory.

May the blessings of the Almighty be upon Your Majesty and your kingdom and may your reign remain peaceful and bring prosperity and unity to your people. Once again we thank Your Majesty for welcoming us to your kingdom and granting us audience.

2

'History Meets Jaja Of Opobo': Introductory Remarks on the Concourse

Tam Fiofori
[Culled from *New Age*, Monday May 23, 2005]

Obviously, when eminent historians meet, history is made, and when these historians in turn interact with a historic figure it naturally becomes an epoch-making event. Between April 30th and 1st May, 2005, *History Concourse 2005, A Celebration of the Life & Work of Professor E.J. Alagoa* was held in Port Harcourt. Various papers were presented by colleagues of Professor Alagoa, including Professors Bolanle Awe (now Pro-Chancellor UNN), Robin Horton, A.E. Afigbo, O.E. Uya, Abdulahi Mahdi, S.I. Udoidem, N.C. Ejituwu and Drs Derefaka, Okorobia and J.H. Enemugwem.

There was also an Art Exhibition featuring P. Abassah, P. Oglafa, D. Tantua and P. Waritimi, music by Timi Ikidi and dance-dramas by TSSK Theatre Company.

On Sunday 1st may, Professor Alagoa (Pro-Chancellor of Niger Delta University, Bayelsa State, as he then was), accompanied by his wife, Hon. Lady M.G. Alagoa JP, his family and participants at the History Concourse 2005 (including writer Dr Gabriel Okara), paid a courtesy visit to

HRM King Dandeson Douglas Jaja JP, Jaja V, Amanyanabo of Opobo, at King Jaja's Palace, Opobo Town, Rivers State.

The guests were received at King Jaja's Jetty and led to the Palace by Alabo G.O.N. Bupo and Alabo Dr S.O.S. Jaja where they met His Majesty in Council. Senibo Bobo Sofiri Brown JP eloquently guided the 'homecoming' reception for Professor Alagoa, regarded as a true friend/'son' of Opobo. Professor Alagoa had many decades back written a book on the famous King Jaja of Opobo and is now a member of the King Jaja Foundation.

Naturally, King Dandeson Jaja, a direct descendant of the world-famous Jaja of Opobo, was delighted to receive Professor Alagoa and his team of visitors. After the Palace reception, group photographs and guided tour, there was an interactive session at the Court Hall, Opobo Town. Senibo Professor B.A. Fubara, Alabo Dr S.O. Jaja. Alabo Professor D.M.J. Fubara, Senibo Professor Winston Bell-Gam and Senibo B.S. Brown presented papers on the history, environment and development of the Opobo Kingdom.

3

Address of Welcome

HRM King Dandeson Douglas Jaja, Jaja V
Amanyanabo of Opobo
[Culled from *New Age*, Monday May 23, 2005]

To be before such eminent historians and personalities, is an honour and for you to have chosen Opobo to be here today, is also an honour. It is an honour to King Jaja of Opobo that Opobo was elected for this historical excursion and the crowning glory of the History Concourse on Professor E.J. Alagoa. You are all very welcome.

Professor E.J. Alagoa's contributions towards King Jaja's history are quite monumental . I remember that he mounted an exhibition on King Jaja at the University of Port Harcourt. It was an exhibition that highlighted so much the contributions of King Jaja to the independence of not only Nigeria, but the Blackman in the diaspora. We are grateful to him.

Recently, I travelled to America and went to the University of California, Los Angeles (UCLA). There I was presented with a book, *The Ways of the Rivers*, and I was pleasantly surprised, very very honoured and proud that Professor E.J. Alagoa was contributor to that monumental book. One of our brothers, Tonye Erekosima, also contributed to the book. Professor Alagoa has done so much for history that we are all very proud of him.

What he has done on King Frederick Koko, [the prosecutor] of [the] Akassa [War], is quite commendable. Unfortunately, our problem is that the leaders of this country have no sense of history. Thank God that we have learnt to honour those that have made contributions to society in their life time. But what about those who had made so much contribution to the history of this country, who have now been forgotten? All their contributions are now in the dustbin of history.

The whitemen came here and our people fought them. In 1895 King Koko fought the Akassa War which they turned to Akassa Raid. It was real war of independence. But nobody remembers him now. Only politicians remember themselves. They make statutes for themselves before they are out of office. But those who made the real contributions are forgotten.

Recently, the burial place of Oba Ovonramwen of Benin was discovered in Calabar. Not even the Federal Government or the State Government of Edo State, took time to honour that man; or to exhume the body and give it a place of honour. Those that genuinely fought for the independence of this country, we are not giving them their rightful and proper place.

How many people read History in the universities these days? Very soon we are not going to have History Professors because we highlight science, the arts and mathematics. We must remember that History is the root of all studies.

I will urge the Professors of History, historians in general, that those our forefathers who fought for the independence of this country should be well documented and remembered. There should be a Hall of Fame for these people. If we do not know from where we started, we may not know our today, neither can we know our future.

King Jaja was whisked away in 1887 from here as a King, and was taken to Accra on trumped-up charges. A panel was then set up and he was banished to the West Indies. All that he did, he did not do for himself alone or Opobo; was to maintain the independence of his city-state. To tell the white man that you cannot come to this place and take over my trade. You can be somewhere and let me give you whatever you want. He was the only man in the Treaty of 1884 who said No and, he would not sign that Treaty until that article was removed. Because, that article attacked his independence.

These are the contributions that men like him have made. We also recall Nana Olomu of the Itsekiris and his fight with the white men over the same trade control. I went to the National Museum in Lagos and I was horrified because there was nothing about these men there, not even their photographs.

This shows that we are losing touch. In Britain they have what they call the National Trust where whole buildings are preserved and the institution takes care of these buildings for posterity. In Opobo Town, we have lost most of our ancient buildings. The present unique statute of King Jaja of Opobo was listed by the National Museums and Antiquities Commission, yet no one comes to inspect and maintain the monument. This shows that our values are misplaced.

If we don't preserve our past, how are we sure our present or the future can be preserved? I am making a personal appeal to historians. You can make things happen in this country. Drum it into the ears of our leaders that we are losing so much that history is leaving us behind and we are not doing what we should do. Our ancestors have done so much. They should be remembered. I feel greatly unhappy when I remember the contributions of these men and, yet they are nowhere now remembered. What we hear now on radio, are the views of our modern politicians who continue to give themselves honours. What they have really contributed, I don't know. The men who have contributed to building this country have been sadly forgotten. This should not be so. This is the duty I am giving to you, today.

4

Past and Present: History and Development in Opobo

S.O. Sunday Jaja

Introduction

We welcome most warmly members of the *History Concourse 2005* to the ancient Kingdom of Opobo. Your visit, we sincerely hope, will not only increase your knowledge of Opobo, help to blend more together the theory, practice and development of Opobo Studies as part of Nigerian history, but, it will, no doubt, open a new era of closer relationship and friendship between History and Historians, especially members of History Concourse and Opobo Kingdom, which you have laboured so hard, individually and collectively to help to build up and explain to other Nigerians and the wide world. We hereby acknowledge all of you and your works on Opobo.

We welcome in particular, Emeritus Professor J.F. Ade Ajayi, one of the Fathers of African History. We assure everyone that he had made so many disciples in the profession of History, built bridges of friendship across the African Continent and beyond. We welcome you to Opobo.

We also welcome Professor (Mrs) Bolanle Awe, one of the Mothers of African History, a mentor and a great teacher of

History. Your disciples in the discipline hold you in very high esteem everywhere in this country and abroad. We wish you more success.

We welcome Professors E.J. Alagoa, A.E. Afigbo, Okon E. Uya, the doyens of African History and the moulders of historical progress, historical methodology and practice across various zones of Nigeria. We appreciate you and wish you more success. We welcome our good friend and brother, Professor N.C. Ejituwu. This is your home. We welcome all other members of the *History Concourse 2005*, and all others and thank you for visiting Opobo today. I was in the team of the Council of the Historical Society of Nigeria that visited the Sultan of Sokoto in 1993 and I have not forgotten my experiences. I was invited to Jaja Village in Sokoto to show our oneness. In the same way, I believe that you will not forget Opobo and the concept of one Nigeria.

Our Debt to the Past and the Present

In 1998 Emeritus Professor A.L.Mabogunje addressed a National Seminar on Environmental Management. His paper was titled "The Debt to Posterity: Reflections on a National Policy on Environmental Management". As usual, it was a very brilliant and illuminating paper prepared and presented to capture the minds and train younger generations of environmental managers in Nigeria. However, the paper never bothered to express any debts to the past or the present. Neither did it mention any debts to history and historians. This approach is understandable. But today, with the members of the History Concourse 2005 before us, one may never be held blameless, if one fails to express our debt, the debt of the entire Opobo people however briefly, to History and Historians, past and present. In view, however, of the time at our disposal, only a few aspects of the debt may be revisited here. And one should be pardoned if all is not said that ought to have been said bearing in mind Carr's (1961) definition of History as a continuous dialogue between the Past and the Present.

Opobo Rediscovered and Given Security and Place in the World

History and Historians have done extremely well in placing Opobo on the world historical map and international affairs from the 19th century to the present day. Since Professor K. Onwuka Dike of blessed memory published his epoch-making book "*Trade and Politics in the Niger Delta*" (1956), Opobo has never been the same again. Dike rediscovered Opobo and removed it from the checklist of colonial casualties and other communities judged, condemned and consigned to the gallows for death in the Niger Delta by colonialists. He brilliantly transferred and placed Opobo in the Hall of Fame and greatness that has survived the vicissitude, the vagaries and the changes and chances of Nigeria's capricious political culture (Cookey, 1974; Alagoa, 1980; Afigbo, 1980; Ajayi, 1985: 10-16). In spite of subsequent change and development in colonial politics, post-independence democratic structures (1960 to 2005), Opobo never lost out in the process. The relevance of Opobo traditional institutions were recognized in the defunct Eastern Nigeria; in the former South Eastern State and Cross River State (1970-1976); and in Rivers State (1997-2005). Kingship and dynastic rule and succession procedure, though temporarily jolted (1980 to 23rd May, 2003) have become firmly rooted and strengthened. The coronation of King Dandeson Douglas Jaja, JP as Jaja V marked the turning down of an unhappy page in the history of Opobo and the confirmation of the historical process of change and development. He is now recognized as First Class Chief and member of Rivers State Council of Chiefs. Your courtesy visit to him is equally historic.

An Ugly Twist

Dike (1956) provided an Appendix called "The Minima Agreement" which he had erroneously termed "Opobo Constitution". From the post-Nigerian civil war years especially, that document nearly tore Opobo Kingdom, its dynastic and traditional institutions apart. Jaja (1991) came readily to hand and explained, through documentary evidence, what seemed to be the reality of the historical situation. But, unfortunately the disputing parties did not listen to the voice and advice of history. Fortunately, a celebrated judgment of Nigeria's Supreme Court (23rd May, 2003) decided the matter and nullified the so called Minima Agreement of 1869. Peace was edified throughout Opobo and the monarchy was restored along with its succession line of kings. A point that has often been emphasized by History and Historians was noted, namely, History can make and unmake a nation or community and point to a new direction. So Historians reserve the right to continue their usual role of using the past to advise the present and warn the future.

Contributions of History and Historians to Other Aspects of Development in Opobo

These are many but a few may be mentioned here.

(a)   Relevance of traditional institutions in Nigeria's democratic process. The Amanyanaboship of Opobo, Opobo Council of Alapu and Opobo/Nkoro Traditional Rulers Council, institutions hallowed by History are still playing important roles in democratic process—peace and security, sufficiency, satisfaction and stimulus—ingredients of development in Opobo communities in line with Curle's (1973) aphorism and criteria for development.

(b)   A new Local Government Area has been achieved—another contribution of History and Historians through the promotion of name, fame and support for pristine greatness,

(c)   Embankment of Opobo foreshores was also granted to support and save Opobo, as a place of History and tourism for Nigeria and the outside world.

(d)   Other developments are now in the pipeline—a new link road to Port Harcourt; electricity through gas turbine and NEPA's national grid (marine cable across Imo River) and so on.

Our Debt to Posterity

History and Historians, we suggest very humbly, still owe a great debt to posterity in Opobo development. One is ashamed to note that until today, there is no full-scale history of Opobo, no Chair of Opobo Studies endowed and the King Jaja Foundation already established has remained dormant. Expansion of Opobo Studies is a task that must be done and quickly too.

Conclusion

We welcome you to historic sites in Opobo. We apologise that some useful sites and buildings have been lost to the Nigerian Civil War or to sheer neglect and lack of a sense of History. We encourage you to see what is available. We assure you that others, which may not be seen on this occasion, will be carefully preserved henceforth to promote historical studies and tourism in Opobo.

# 5

Environmental Issues of Concern in Opobo Kingdom

Dagogo M.J. Fubara, JP

1.0 Summary of the Environmental Factors

Opobo Kingdom as an integral part of the Niger Delta, is beset with several environmental problems. The causative factors include:

(i) The Niger Delta natural ecology and physical environmental characteristics of low lying, flat, swampy terrain criss-crossed by a myriad of rivers and creeks, aggravated by excessive rainfall of about 4000mm/year which falls over nine of the twelve months of the year. These peculiar conditions of the Niger Delta make infrastructural development cost up to more than TEN times the cost in other parts of Nigeria.

(ii) Man-made problems arising from non-sustainable and destructive economic activities, especially those of oil and gas industry, without necessary and adequate remedial protection and restoration of the environment made oppressive by the lack of political goodwill and justice required for redress through RESOURCE CONTROL in TRUE FEDERALISM or equitable revenue allocation for adequate investment in socio-economic infrastructural development and environmental protection. The Colonial Government recognized this need when it instituted the payment of COMEY SUBSIDIES to coastal kingdoms like Opobo since the mid-1800s.

(iii)   Unjust and oppressive petroleum industry regulatory laws and the Land Use Act now entrenched in the Constitution

2.0   Specifics of the Environmental Issues

These problems include:

2.1   Building the Aluminium Smelting Company of Nigeria (ALSCON) and its dredging of the lower Imo River (Opobo River) without compliance with the legal stipulations for an Environmental Impact Assessment (EIA) report acceptable to all neighbouring stakeholders as provided for in FEPA EIA Decree 86 of 1992. On this issue, Opobo Community protests to:

(a)   The Honourable Minister of Power and Steel
(b)   Honourable Minister of Environment
(c)   The Managing Director of ALSCON
(d)   The Director of National Inland Waterways Authority

have been ignored without the simple courtesy of ordinary acknowledgement. ALSCON ocean liners using the lower Opobo River as shipping route will generate waves that will aggravate erosion and pose serious danger to small river crafts currently in use for passenger and commercial transport.

2.2 Rapid loss of the little habitable land (less than 20% of the environment) due to shore line erosion is devastating Kalama, Queenstown and Kalaibiama communities of Opobo Kingdom.

2.3 The total collapse of the Queenstown shoreline protection embankment despite the fact that the collapsing signal started in early 1990 and for which the inhabitants raised all the necessary alarm to the Federal Government and OMPADEC for intervention and remedial work is extremely demoralizing.

2.4 The lack of "toe erosion" monitoring and cathodic maintenance protection of the Opobo Town steel sheet piling protection embankment require immediate attention to prevent the collapse of that embankment with its consequent disastrous impact.

2.5 The abandonment of the Opobo Town backswamp reclamation and drainage scheme initiated by OMPADEC to save Opobo Town from flooding through the backswamp and the reclaiming of land for the town's habitable land expansion is an urgent issue for NDDC to redress without further delay.

2.6 NYPAPALM vegetation rapid expansion has all but made extinct the natural Niger Delta vegetation of mangrove forest. The attendant result includes accelerated shorebank erosion; destruction of shell fishery development and harvesting which is a lucrative economic activity; rivercraft transportation hazard due to engine propeller damage by the large floating seeds of this palm.

2.7 The exploration and production activities of the oil and gas industry cause several serious environmental concerns such as indiscriminate destruction of marine wild life and fisheries by seismic operations and pollution from oil spillages that also adversely affect human health, ecological damage, including corroding acid rain caused by gas flaring and whose penalty incomes are paid to the Federal Government rather than the affected community.

In this regard, it is pertinent to reproduce the following remarks which General Kotangora who in 1989, as Nigeria's Federal Minister of Works and Housing and who was then responsible for environmental matters, said:

> "The oil industry has undoubtedly brought economic benefits to many of our people but it has also left in it's trail, a complex mix of environmental, political and socio-economic problems."

The Nigeria National report to the United Nations Conference on Environment and Development (UNCED) 1992, summarized the details of these environmental and socio-economic problems as follows:

> "Coastal Marine Pollution: The coastal and marine environment have been impaired by continuous input of domestic sewage,

industrial effluents, petroleum hydrocarbons, dredged material and garbage. These have reduced the value of the aquatic resources for recreation (swimming, bathing, etc.), fisheries (artisanal and industrial) and transportation. The decline in quality of near shore waters is expressed by oily sheen and discoloration due to heavy suspended matter. These effects are aggravated by rapid urbanization and exploration in the Niger Delta Area. The coastal belt is especially vulnerable to frequent oil spills, which have adverse effects on fish stock, wildlife, and the fragile mangrove ecosystems. Other potential problems arising from our low lying geosyncline are saltwater intrusion and land subsidence both of which are accelerated by developments in the oil and gas industry."

2.7.1 Lesson from Mobil Oil Spillage

In spite of the above, it is painful to note the reaction of Mobil, after the Mobil Oil Spill from Mobil IDOHO facility on OML68, about 20km South of Qua Iboe River and 45km Southeast of Imo River (Opobo River) estuary, when our fishermen and women reported sighting widespread oily sheen throughout the aforesaid offshore fishing grounds, the sandy beaches of that coastal zone and its creeks and adjacent mangrove swamps. They also reported numerous dead fishes and marine life, some floating offshore and in the creeks, while others lay on the beaches and in the mangrove swamps. They equally reported the absence of the usual numerous schools of fish in these fishing grounds, leading to drastic reduction in their catches and its attendant devastation of their economic life.

The scientific interplay between the environmental and ecologic damages due to oil spillage, on the one hand, and the sighting of dead fishes and other marine life including birds and the absence of fish and loss of fish catches on the other hand is a well known world-wide phenomenon. Besides, it would take these fishing grounds several years to recover from this environmental damage because not only have the full grown fishes died, but most importantly, the unseen fishes fingerlings and marine life eggs and larvae that would produce new ones have been irrevocably destroyed by the impact of the oil spill.

Our fishermen and those engaged in fish processing and sales derive their livelihood from the near offshore zone fishing grounds stretching from the estuaries of the Qua Iboe River through those of Imo River (Opobo River), Andoni River to Bonny River, and the stretch of the rest of the Nigerian coastal zone and inland estuarine creeks westward to the Lagos Lagoon.

The main economic activities of these coastal zone dwellers are almost solely dependent on fisheries and marine life. Thus, the entire population of the Nigerian coastal zone has been economically strangulated now and for many years to come.
These facts should be well known from the adverse environmental impacts of oil spillages, be they in Alaska,

USA, Canada, Japan or South East Asia. Nevertheless, we notice that the focus of the basis for environmental damage claim has been shifted by Mobil Department for Environmental and Loss Prevention to requiring fishermen to produce oil-damaged fishing gears.

This is a very unfair, unjust and mischievous play on the intelligence of these ill-informed fishermen and the affected coastal zone communities, by taking undue advantage of their scientific ignorance by Mobil. Mobil Producing Unlimited must pay fair and just compensation for the environmental and ecological damage according to international convention to prevent further violent agitations affecting other companies and peace in the Niger Delta and Nigeria.

2.7.2 Lesson from Oil Production as Non-Renewable Resource: The case of Oloibiri

Oloibiri, the mother of Nigeria's crude oil production, which is no longer producing crude oil, is now barren, with destroyed ecosystem so impoverished and without any life supporting infrastructure that nobody can associate it with Nigeria's first crude oil production of 1956. It is now about twenty (20) years since the Federal Government widely publicized but has failed to build an oil museum at Oloibiri to improve the income generation of the poverty stricken community.

2.7.3 Repressive Oil Industry Regulatory Laws

A number of the nation's regulatory laws and agencies detract from the efforts to mitigate Niger Delta environmental problems so as to promote sustainable development. Some of the statutes regulating the petroleum industry activities and community rights are unfair, unjust, and inequitable for the interest of sustainable development of the Niger Delta and other mineral and gas producing States. These statutes, which should be amended to eliminate injustice, include:

(i) Petroleum Decree 1969 (now Act of 1990) as amended
(ii) Oil Terminal Dues Act
(iii) Oil terminal Act
(iv) Land Use Decree of 1978
(v) Exclusive Economic Zone Act of 1978
(vi) Associated Gas Re-Injection Act of 1979
(vii) Oil Pipelines and Lands (Title Vestings etc.) Decree No. 52 of 1993
(viii) National Inland Waterways Authority Decree No. 13 of 1997

These laws deny us the natural rights to the funds needed to develop the harsh environment of the Niger Delta. It is only in Nigeria that Rents and Royalties are not paid to the producing communities but to the Federal Government. This should also be reversed.

The composition of FEPA hierarchy is badly deficient of federal character. Consequently, FEPA did not represent the interest of the Niger Delta and hence Rivers State at the United Nations Conference on Environment and Development

(UNCED), Rio de Janeiro, 1992, and follow on UN conferences. Even when the World Bank, as a result of Ada George/Peter Odili sponsored report to UNCED, decided to undertake sustainable environmental developmental programmes for the Niger Delta, FEPA scuttled the World Bank plan.

Also FEPA's enforcement of the provisions of the Environmental Impact Assessment (EIA) Decree 86 of 1992 is highly defective. To merely display an EIA report for twenty days for sighting at only FEPA designated offices without an independent expert panel review and adequate public hearing prevents the use of EIA for effective environmental protection. Because of intensive industrial activities in the Niger Delta over 95% of all EIA reports are produced for the Niger Delta. The present casual treatment of EIA reports is not in the best interest of the Niger Delta environmental protection and conservation.

2.8 The British Colonial Government appreciated the sustainable developmental needs of the Niger Delta and its inhabitants before Nigeria's independence in 1960. This arose from the submissions of the Rivers Chiefs and Peoples Conference led by Late Chief (Dr) Harold Dappa Biriye at the Nigerian Constitutional Conference of 1957 in London. As a result, the Willink's Commission of Inquiry was set up for the Protection of Minority Rights and Interest in Nigeria but this protection is yet to be achieved. The Willink's Commission Report observed as follows:

"We were impressed by the arguments indicating that the needs of those who lived in the creeks and swamps of the Niger Delta are very different from those of the interior. We agree that it is not easy for a Government or a Legislature operating far from inland to concern itself, or even fully understand the problems of a territory where communications are so difficult, building so expensive and education so scanty. That, however, is not to say that a separate state is the best means of achieving the ends desired by the people of the creek."

The Willink Commission sought to defend their rejection of the claim for separate statehood on these further grounds. They said in a concluding part of their Report:

"We cannot recommend political arrangements which would unite in one political unit the whole body of Ijaws...We suggest that there should be a Federal board appointed to consider the problems of the area of the Niger Delta ..."

Before granting independence to Nigeria, the British Government therefore proposed that the Niger Delta be declared "A Special Federal Territory" for focused development. However, due to the strong opposition of Nigerian leaders, Niger Delta was not made a Federal Territory but a special development area for which the Niger Delta Development Board was created. This board failed to achieve any desired results due to structural defects and lack of political goodwill, fairness and justice in revenue allocation and lack of independence and executive powers.

By 1958, the area defined as the natural Niger Delta now consists of , from West to East, the States of Delta, Bayelsa, Rivers and Akwa-Ibom. At that time the Niger Delta basic developmental problems arose from natural adverse environmental characteristics, which demand unusual injection of funds to achieve normal socio-economic and infrastructural development. Since then, these have been further compounded by man-made industrial hazards, particularly from the petroleum and gas industry.

The Principle of Derivation has been consciously, systematically and unjustly manipulated by successive regimes of the Federal Government from 100% (1953) to 50% (1960) shortly after crude oil production and exportation began in 1958, to 30% (1970), 25% (1977), 0% (1979-1981), 1.5% (1982) to 3% (1992) and not less than 13% (1999 to date). In 1953 the areas of derivation was paid 100% Rents/Royalties. This was reduced to 50% in 1964. By 1964, the regions started arguing about factors like population and land mass but Binn observed that the overall environmental devastation and health hazard caused by petroleum exploration and exploitation activities demanded that the region of origin should have nothing less than 50%. Furthermore, Binn queried the 20% Federal share by Raisman and returned to the 15% Federal share suggested in 1951 by Hicks-Phillipson. This formula remained in force till 1970 and was practiced as a workable formula by the regions and later 12 states (from 1967).

Past myopic philosophy and lack of political goodwill, fairness and justice, equity and sensitivity in governance are exemplified by a former Federal Permanent Secretary, later Director of Chevron Oil Company and eventually Secretary for Petroleum Resources in Babaginda's Transition Government, who in a public lecture in 1980, said:

> "... there is a long way to go to meet the claims of the oil producing areas which see themselves as losing non-replaceable resources while replaceable and permanent resources of agriculture and industry are being developed elsewhere largely with oil revenue. Given, however, the small size and population of the oil producing areas, it is cynical to observe that even if the resentments of the oil producing areas continue, they cannot threaten the stability of the country nor affect its economic development."

Current events and their impacts have proved him wrong. Such insensitivity and wrong leadership vision created the problems of the Niger Delta that must now be redressed not only to be fair and just to the Niger Delta dwellers but to prevent further threat to the stability of our country and our economic activities. Unfortunately, he like most Nigerians from the non-oil producing areas, resent, with great sense of injustice and unfair play, any effort to redress the Niger Delta episode. They are unwilling to recognize and/or understand the linkages and interplay between oil mineral and gas exploitation and ecological degradation, which necessitates large injection of funds for rehabilitation and redress management for sustainable development of the endangered Niger Delta. Some of the policy pronouncements of a former Special Adviser to the Head of State lend credence to this perpetrated insensitivity of the Federal Government.

3. **Redress of the Environmental issues:**
    President Obasanjo's Redress Prescription

The answers to these issues of peace and development in Nigeria in general and, the Niger Delta in particular or the necessary redress management and sustainable developmental objectives have been aptly enunciated by H.E. Olusegun Obasanjo (GCFR) himself, the President, Commander-in-Chief of the Armed Forces of the Federal Republic of Nigeria in his various addresses. In particular, he prescribed the philosophy for his governance objectives as follows, at the inception of his administration.

> The return to True Federalism, where the various strata; Federal, State and Local Governments relate to each other according to the spirit of the constitution.

> A society governed by laws and the observance of universally accepted standards of moral and ethical behaviour by public servants and the citizenry.

A country where things work—no fuel scarcity, there should be regular power supply, reliable communications, efficient public transportation and functional infrastructural capacity which is continually upgraded to anticipate the growing requirements of a virile economy.

A buoyant economy, full employment and full security for all and a proper balance of public and private sector activities.

The integrated development of rural areas such that every where in Nigeria will have basic amenities—light, water, schools, good roads and good health facilities etc.

A safe and secure environment for persons and property.

Efficient and service-oriented social services.

The sustainable development of human resources through sound education.

The development of the Niger Delta, other oil producing areas and the segments of the country affected by ecological and/or environmental degradation.

These are undoubtedly the required fundamentals for excellent, just, fair and equitable governance for national reconstruction to make Nigeria rise again.

Therefore, to redress some of these issues and accomplish the President's prescription will require:

(a) The amendment of the 1999 Constitution to effect TRUE FEDERALISM and enforce TRUE FEDERAL FISCAL policy and the principle of RESOURCE CONTROL which King Jaja of Opobo fought for and for which the British Government deported him in 1887.

(b) Adoption of the principles in the 1993 UN Law of the Sea Convention and the definition of coastal state rights in the continental shelf as per the 1960 Constitution.

In addition to the above, as an integral part of the Niger Delta, for the Opobo Kingdom in particular, the environmental issues of concern raised in Sections 2.1 to 2.8 whose redress is both implicitly and explicitly obvious need to be tackled immediately. The problems of utmost urgency which the Niger Delta Development Commission (NDDC) should tackle, immediately are (i) the Opobo Town backswamp reclamation project of OMPADEC, now abandoned, (ii) the restoration of the collapsed Queenstown embankment, and (iii) foreshore erosion protection of KALAMA community.

The Concept of Resource Control in Correct Perspective

There has been an unfair distortion of the concept of RESOURCE CONTROL in order to kill it unjustly. TRUE FEDERALISM demands TRUE FISCAL policy, which includes

RESOURCE CONTROL, practiced in the progressive democratic countries. RESOURCE CONTROL does NOT mean "winner take all". It means control of the means and mode of production in a sustainable way. For example, for the oil and gas industry in Nigeria, it means that an establishment like NNPC is controlled by the state/provincial governments of the indigenous natural owners of the area of exploitation and production. The resultant revenue is taxed according to world-wide practice and the sum realized is then paid into the Federation Account. The indigenous natural owners then use their share of the resources revenue to develop, protect and conserve their environment.

6

Towards the Sustainable Development of Opobo

Winston I. Bell-Gam

I   **Historical Notes**

Opobo Kingdom was established on December 25, 1870 by Ibani Chiefs and their War Canoe Houses that eluded Grand Bonny in 1869.

Its development goals at that time were dictated by the exigencies of its origin:

- Need for adequate military defence force
- Need for adequate space for the physical establishment of the town
- Need to obtain and retain competitive advantage in the oil trade of the time.

Accomplishment of these gaols was rapidly achieved and Opobo became a thriving Kingdom made up of a main town and several satellite towns with settlements of various sizes.

Several factors helped establish the kingdoms competitive advantage as a trading city-state. These are:

(i) The site of the City-State of Opobo with the satellite towns had a significant locational advantage (the mouth of the Imo River whose arterial system constituted the main routes to several inland settlements).

(ii) A natural harbour, which needed only operational dredging maintenance.

(iii) A stable administrative (governance) machinery pivoted on the War Canoe House structure—a sort of federation of War canoe Houses with a ruling Monarch (Amanyanabo).

(iv) Arising from interaction with early missionaries and colonialists, a large resource of educated citizens.

(v) The traditional occupation of fishing led to the creation of several fishing ports, the point of origin of many thriving towns in the Niger Delta.

(vi) The powerful entrepreneurial Chiefs that founded and ran their various War Canoe Houses which some have described as large commercial cooperatives.

II Combination of Environmental and Changing Economic Scenarios Which Led to the Decline of the Economy and Influence of the City-State

The glory of Opobo Kingdom like those of several other City-States of the Niger Delta dwindled to exceedingly low levels for a number of reasons, leaving behind memories of a glorious past seen in the uniform layout of the towns and settlements, several monuments of sculptor and stone-covered graves, and governance machinery that is exemplary as it represents perhaps one of the earliest traditional systems of governance based on the rule of law in Nigeria. The constraints to the development have been documented as:

(a) Land resources are in short supply and should be adequately improved and managed.
(b) Sand bars development constitutes an important constraint on the navigation of the rivers and creeks and a barrier to development of ports for shipping and fishing.
(c) Poor soils make development difficult and expensive.
(d) Salinity of marsh soils have kept our conventional agriculture from the area.
(e) Lack of transportation and other communications infrastructure has stagnated all types of economic/commercial development.
(f) Lack of water and electricity for domestic industrial use.

The general thrust of sustainable development in Opobo Kingdom has to be dictated by the need to reverse the listed constraints so as to re-establish social services, economic, commercial and industrial activities. This will require the production of a resource map for the area. Such resource map is a vital requirement for the selection and location of appropriate industries.

- The building of appropriate infrastructure is a *sine qua non* for sustainable development.
- Environmental problems are challenges to sustainable development and known to include:
  - agricultural land degradation
  - flooding
  - fisheries depletion

- deforestation
- biodiversity loss
- nypa palm proliferation
- toxic and hazardous substances
- sewage
- vehicular emissions
- municipal solid waste
- oil pollution

To arrest the effects of environmental problems, development goals must be expanded to include the preparation and adoption of an environmental management plan—details of which are excluded from this brief presentation.

III   The Development Partners

Government (Federal, State and Local) is the main organ for the development of Opobo Kingdom. The deficiency in government delivered facilities has precipitated the need for other stakeholders to join as partners for sustainable development.

The major stakeholders, the oil companies and NGOs are now becoming active participants in the development of Opobo Kingdom.

IV   Blue Print for Sustainable Development

The Amanyanabo and the Chiefs of Opobo in Council has established a Think Tank Committee with the mandate to produce a Sustainable Development Blueprint for the Kingdom.

The multi-disciplinary group of citizens is in the process of producing the document. This document contains a more detailed overview of the development aspira'ons, possibilities and strategies for the Kingdom. The advantage of a focused leadership has been demonstrated by the Chiefs. The State Government has the responsibility of providing roads, electricity and water. The Local Government, the industrial stakeholders, NGOs and entrepreneurs must respond adequately to these when they become available. It is notable that the Governor of Rivers State, Dr Peter Odili recently unveiled the 'foundation stone' of the Ogoni-Andoni-Opobo Road.

Successful completion of this road will unveil new dimensions of development, which can only be imagined at this stage.

7

A New Local Economy to Re-Invent Opobo Kingdom: Notes on a Development Model for the Niger Delta and Other Zones of Nigeria

Bobo Sofiri Brown, JP

1. Overview

We begin this conversation with an accusation. Nigerian historians appear to have been on vacation for too long. Perhaps more than ever before, Nigeria needs them to go back to serious work. They need to help our nation pay deeper attention to the history of its people in a way to better handle the present challenges of national development.

The history of Opobo Kingdom offers two strong reasons for an extended engagement with Nigeria's past. First is that in 1869 the founding fathers or pioneer Chiefs of Opobo, embarked on a resolute journey in search of something new: a kingdom to match their dream. The City-State they established on December 25, 1870 soon achieved an enviable position. It became one of the exemplary development landmarks of pre-colonial Nigeria.

How did the people translate such a dream into reality, one notable as a resounding success story within a relatively short time? What did they do that made the difference in handling the challenges that confronted the coastal areas of what was to become Nigeria? We need objective answers to such questions. The effort to provide answers will encourage a proper focus on the fundamental elements of "state craft" in our hardworking and creative ancient kingdoms and communities. This is opposed to the new culture of "state graft" in contemporary unproductive Nigeria.

The second reason for a closer engagement with Opobo history, carries a ring of urgency. This is due to the current pressure of globalization on countries, communities and other people. The actual balance sheet of globalization is not noticed easily. It creates "winners" and "losers" through the market place which brings unequal players together. This is because of the role of modern communications in advancing the ideology of consumerism. It does not highlight that those who only consume without comparative productivity, are structurally "losers" in the global market.

Opobo Kingdom resisted the role of "losers" in the encounter with mercantilist Europe. It became an active and productive player in the market. Nigeria can learn a lot from this history as it grapples with globalization.

2. A Market in Your Face

The role of modern communications in the new world is at the heart of globalization. It is worth our brief attention here. Generally, communication makes business possible at all. But today communications is facilitating the relentless integration of distant nooks and corners into the international market place. The interesting point is that the process wears an innocuous appearance as news, data or entertainment. Cable, satellite TV and Internet bring the glamour of American film stars and life styles, Japanese industrial goods and nude beach parties in Hawaii into our living rooms here. Whether in Ikare-Ekiti, Igbere, Mubi, Abak, Abonnema or King Jaja's Palace, at the mere push of a button the world is in your face. But this essentially brings the market into your bedroom, without your feeling so.

The effect of what appears to be entertainment or news is clear in countries where people can buy and sell through the phone or Internet. Here is Africa far from the e-commerce high way of the global market, the effect takes a little time to manifest. We find that our decisions of what to buy are somehow influenced by what we have seen on Cable TV, Video, Internet or real life colour pages of publications.

This is "visual messaging". The world of "show me" persuades you into action through what you see. This technique is not really new in the market place. The early European traders on the coastal kingdoms of pre-colonial Nigeria deployed it to win customers for their goods. Opobo thus became a centre for the consumption of expensive high-end foreign goods such as imported monuments, pre-fab mansions and public buildings (e.g. churches). The difference is that Opobo Kingdom matched consumption of such goods with an increasing productive role in trade with Europe. Even more, it consumed goods that endured in shaping the society.

3. Why a Local Economy?

Images of the Niger Delta present a form of illusion as reality. A good example is Opobo Kingdom. When you read the inspiring history and accounts of its founding fathers led by Africa's illustrious statesman King Jaja of Opobo, you see images of the Kingdom. A visit such as this or a TV documentary on Opobo, presents you with concrete structures and other appearances that create images of "progress". Yet the reality is different.

So what went wrong? The local economy of the palm oil era collapsed. This was worsened by the advent of the crude oil and gas economy, which became the kingdom's second encounter with an oil economy. Unfortunately, the new oil economy has no productive role for indigenous communities. Its operations tend to destroy any productive potentials through several punitive and exploitative regulations or the capital intensive technology of the business. Where these fail, the oppressive machinery of state power is visited on the oil and gas communities to facilitate maximum revenue to be shared by those in power in Abuja etc.

The collapse of the local economies of the Niger Delta, has led to subsequent collapse of social institutions and governance systems that were built on it. Mass unemployment and massive poverty in this region have been rated as the highest in Nigeria by a recent study. Stampede for daily survival has become a regular experience. The result is tension and violence that manifest the loss of a viable local economy.

4.   An Alternative View

For years the Niger Delta has received many pious sympathisers from inside and outside Nigeria. But no one has done anything about positive realignment of the local economies to the macro oil and gas economy. This has led to communities taking up negative alignment of a long drawn struggle with oil and gas companies. Recently the struggle has gone one step higher with elementary bunkering activities by some indigenes. Unfortunately they are too weak financially and politically to compete against the major oil thieves who are largely protected by state power.

We face the influx of NGOs and the arrogance of the oil companies that play "god father" in the Niger Delta. Despite huge millions of US dollars allegedly spent on community development in the Niger Delta, not one community can boast of a viable local economy. Even worse, the communities are prostrate, dependent, poverty stricken and therefore crisis prone. They remain victims of the new oil economy.

An alternative model is thus necessary. It is to re-engineer the local economies into an integrated regional productivity pool. Thus communities would share in productive activities that draw from the comparative advantage of each local economy. Those that mass produce a particular raw material can be linked by processing plants in their neighbourhood. Both groups are further linked to packaging and marketing centres within their zones. One zone or region can then become a supplier of some products to other zones in the country while consuming products from those zones. Such internal interdependence will provide the basic economic energy to compete in the global market. But a clear imagery of who we want to be has to inform the design of our local economies.

5. Conclusion

To re-invent Opobo Kingdom is therefore a challenge to first dream and create the imagery that will provide "visual messaging" of who we want to be. Then a determined effort to positively re-align the local economy will follow. From the two interactions a new reality will emerge to make the place a vibrant and proud kingdom all over again. This is the model the Niger Delta desires for its true development. History says it can be done, because it has been done before in this land.

The local economy that created a competitive advantage and prosperity for the Kingdom is no more. The palm produce trade was the kingdom's first encounter with the oil economy. Opobo faced an acute disadvantage in terms of lack of farmlands and agricultural skill to produce palm oil and kernels for European markets. But the kingdom became a platform for ingenuity and high entrepreneurship in the palm oil economy. The drive to participate in the oil economy and to secure a niche in it, moved the founding Chiefs away from their homeland in Grand Bonny in 1869. For many of them were not involved in the communal crisis between Jaja and Oko-Jumbo in Bonny. They joined the exodus to Opobo to take advantage of access to the hinterland market which the new kingdom offered.

There is a lesson for today's Resource Control champions of our Niger Delta. It is not just the control of revenue that matters. It is even more important in a "show me" world, to put such revenue to productive and profitable use which all can see. But to do so calls for an imagery of positive reality that we wish to create. Thus there is a need to positively align the local economy to the macro economy by utilizing available resources to give the human and material assets in the communities competitive advantage. Opobo Kingdom did so in the 19th century. Its conscious role in the palm oil economy sustained governance, social, cultural and religious structures/values to ensure internal stability and progress of the citizenry. Even more, the kingdom invested in the "future", with early procurement of high-end indigenous and European goods such as "Gigs", "Ekere", Monuments, Cannons and Education etc. which helped to project the cultural and social identity of Opobo Kingdom.

HISTORY CONCOURSE 2005
ATTENDANCE REGISTER

Professor A E **Afigbo,** Department of History & International Relations, Ebonyi State University, Abakaliki; Home Address: P O Box 734, Okigwe, Omo State [0803-265 4579]

Lady Mercy G **Alagoa,** 11 Orogbum Crescent, GRA Phase II, Port Harcourt [0803-716 5277]

Mrs Ibiere D **Alagoa**, 11 Orogbum Crescent, GRA Phase II, Port Harcourt

Professor E J **Alagoa,** 11 Orogbum Crescent, GRA Phase II, Port Harcourt [0803-308 3385]

Johnbull **Amasibo,** 127 Niger Street, Port Harcourt [0803-268 3937]

Rev S T K **Appah,** Niger Delta University, Wilberforce Island, Bayelsa State [0803-756 5726]

Professor Bolanle **Awe,** Pro-Chancellor, University of Nigeria, Nsukka

Lindsay **Barrett,** Imiringi, Bayelsa State

Dr A A **Derefaka,** Department of History & Diplomatic Studies, University of Port Harcourt, Choba [0803-342 2133]

Chief O G S **Digbani,** Almarine Co. Ltd, Plot 28 Kolokuma Street, Borikiri, Port Harcourt [0803-583 8685]

Akanimo O **Ebong,** 1 Yenagoa Street, Delta Park, University of Port Harcourt, Choba [0802-742 9884]

Professor N C **Ejituwu,** Department of History & Diplomatic Studies, University of Port Harcourt, Choba [0803-338 3480]

Dr John H **Enemugwem,** Department of History & Diplomatic Studies, University of Port Harcourt, Choba

Tam **Fiofori,** P O Box 2788, Surulere, Lagos [0803-313 4007]

Robin **Horton,** Oribo Polo, Buguma [0803-708 1564]

John **Ighodaro,** State Correspondent, Vanguard Medici Ltd, Port Harcourt

Timipa E J **Igoli,** Department of History & Diplomatic Studies, University of Port Harcourt, Choba [0803-708 4847]

Stella **Inametti,** NTA Correspondent, Port Harcourt [0803-312 4307]

Ifeanyi **Izeze,** New Age Newspaper, Port Harcourt [0803-304 3009]

Dr Jones M **Jaja,** Institute of Foundation Studies, Rivers State University of Science & Technology, Port Harcourt [0803-316 8998]

Abdullahi **Mahadi,** Gombe State University, PMB 127, Gombe [234-072 20099]

Dennis **Naku,** Champion Newspapers, 47 Ikwerre Road, Port Harcourt [0805-673 8559]

Ndubueze **Nwankwo,** NTA Premises, Port Harcourt

Hon Fred **Nyananyo,** 16 Alexander Avenue, Rumuokwuta, Port Harcourt [0803-711 3969]

Ruby Iwoyefa **Nyananyo** [0803-322 8385]

Richard **Obomanu,** Department History & Diplomatic Studies, University of Port Harcourt, Choba [0803-339 1205]

Dr Gabriel I G **Okara,** 10 Ndoni Close, Abuloma Housing Estate, Port Harcourt [0803-708 3538]

Dr A M **Okorobia,** Department of History & Diplomatic Studies, University of Port Harcourt, Choba [0802-318 4635]

Odudu **Okpongete,** Daily Independent Newspaper, Port Harcourt [0805-304 0239]

Samuel **Onuche,** Art Source, 3 Njemanze Street, Port Harcourt [0803-310 8013]

Dr Kingdom E **Orji,** Department of Humanities, Rivers State College of Arts & Science, P M B 5936, Port Harcourt [0805-666 9109]

Sereba Agiobu-Kemmer **Pearse** [0803-340 0057]

Christopher **Peters,** 61 Woji. Road, GRA Phase II, Port Harcourt   [0803-342 6562]

Usen Ubom **Stanilus,** Department of Chemical Engineering, University of Port Harcourt, Choba   [0803-675 3623]

Beemene N **Taneh,** No. 37 Worukwo Street, Port Harcourt

Ebitari **Tekenah,** 11 Orogbum Crescent, GRA Phase II, Port Harcourt

Ms Ruth **Tekenah,** 11 Orogbum Crescent, GRA Phase II, Port Harcourt

Professor S I **Udoidem,** Dean, Faculty of Humanities, Port Harcourt, Choba

Okon E **Uya,** Department of History and International Studies, University of Calabar, Calabar; [0803-265 4579]
E-mail: okoneuya@yahoo.co.uk

Okwakpam **Weguma,** NTA Premises, Port Harcourt

CHAPTER REFERENCES
and Select Bibliography
Compiled by
Jigekuma A. Ombu

I. REFERENCES

CHAPTER 2. ALAGOA: THE PHILOSOPHER

1. E.J. Alagoa, "The Relationship between history and other disciplines, " *Tarikh*, Vol. 6 No. 1, 1978-1980, p. 12-80.
2. E.J. Alagoa, *The Uses of Hindsight as Foresight*. Port Harcourt: Onyoma Research Publications, 2004, p. vi.
3. E.J. Alagoa, *The Uses of Hindsight as Foresight*, p.v.
4. E.J. Alagoa, *The Uses of Hindsight as Foresight, p. vi.*
5. E.J. Alagoa, *The Uses of Hindsight as Foresight, p. 66.*
6. Inculturation is here understood as the act and the process by which a new reality emerges from an old one. The image that can help to explain this process is that of a hatching egg that brings forth a chick. What comes out is not the yolk of the egg. It is something different and yet without the egg (yolk) there would be no chick.
7. E.J. Alagoa, *More Days, More Wisdom: Nembe Proverbs,* Ibadan: University of Ibadan Press, 1986, pp. 48-49.
8. E.J. Alagoa, *More Days, More Wisdom: Nembe Proverbs,* 30-31.

9   E.J. Alagoa, "An African Philosophy of Time," In Sulayman Bachir Diagne & Heinz Kimmerle (Editors). *Time and Development in the Thought of Sub-Saharan Africa: Studies in Intercultural Philosophy*, Vol. 8, 1998, p. 220.

10   E.J. Alagoa, "African Philosophy of Time," *Time and Development in the Thought of Sub-Saharan Africa*, p. 221.

11   E.J. Alagoa, "African Philosophy of Time," *Time and Development in the Thought of Sub-Saharan Africa*, p. 221.

12   E.J. Alagoa, *The Uses of Hindsight as Foresight*, p.2.

13   E.J. Alagoa, *The Uses of Hindsight as Foresight*, p. 4.

14   E.J. Alagoa, *The Uses of Hindsight as Foresight*, p. 12.

15   E.J. Alagoa, *The Uses of Hindsight as Foresight*, p. 20.

16   E.J. Alagoa, *The Uses of Hindsight as Foresight*, p. 11-12.

17   E.J. Alagoa, "African Philosophy of Time," *Time and Development in the Thought of Sub-Saharan Africa*, p. 218.

18   R.K. Ryan, *The Confessions of St. Augustine*, New York: Image Books, 1960, pp. 298.

19   E.J. Alagoa, *The Uses of Hindsight as Foresight*, p. 139.

20   E.J. Alagoa, "African Philosophy of Time," *Time and Development in the Thought of Sub-Saharan Africa*, p. 218.

21   R.K. Ryan, *The Confessions of St. Augustine*, New York: Image Books, 1960, pp. 287-300.

22 E.J. Alagoa, "African Philosophy of Time," *Time and Development in the Thought of Sub-Saharan Africa*, p. 218.

23 R.K. Ryan, *The Confessions of St. Augustine,* New York: Image Books, 1960, pp. 287.

24 John S. Mbiti, *African Religions and Philosophy*, London: Heinemann, 1969, p. 17; 73.

25 John A.A. Ayoade, "Time in Yoruba Thought" In *African Philosophy: An Introduction*, 2nd Edition. Richard A. Wright (ed.) Maryland, Lanham: University Press of America, 1984. pp. 71-89.

26 E.J. Alagoa, *More Days More Wisdom: Nembe Proverbs*, pp. 48-49.

27 E.J. Alagoa, *More Days, More Wisdom: Nembe Proverbs*, pp. 30-31.

28 E.J. Alagoa, *More Days, More Wisdom: Nembe Proverbs*, pp. 30-31.

29 E.J. Alagoa, "African Philosophy of Time," *Time and Development in the Thought of Sub-Saharan Africa*, p. 220.

30 E.J. Alagoa, *More Days More Wisdom: Nembe Proverbs*, p. 89.

31 E.J. Alagoa, "The Encounter Between African and Western Historiography Before 1800," In *Storia Della Storiografia*, Vol. 19, 1991, p. 74.

32 E.J. Alagoa, *The Uses of Hindsight as Foresight,* p. 6.

33 E.J. Alagoa, *The Uses of Hindsight as Foresight,* p. 142-143.

34 E.J. Alagoa, "Prof. E.J. Alagoa, Professor of History" in *This I Believe: The Philosophies and Personal Histories of 24 Eminent Nigerian Achievers*, Edited by Dipo Ajayi. Lagos: Prestige Associates, pp. 63-72.

CHAPTER 3: ALAGOA: ORAL TRADITION AND THE MULTI-METHOD APPROACH

1. For the lessons he drew from this work, see his: *Oral Tradition*. London: Routledge and Kegan Paul, 1965.

2. E.J. Alagoa, *A History of the Niger Delta*. Ibadan: Ibadan University Press, 1972. E.J. Alagoa, F.N. Anozie and N. Nzewunwa (eds.), *The Early History of the Niger Delta*. Hamburg: Helmut Buske Verlag, 1988.

3. D.P. Henige, *The Chronology of Oral Tradition*. Oxford: Clarendon Press, 1974.

4. R. Horton, "Ancient Ife: A Reassessment", *Journal of the Historical Society of Nigeria*, Vol. 9, No. 4, 1979.

5. R. Horton, "Some Fresh Thoughts on Eastern Ijọ Origins, Expansions and Migrations", in N.C. Ejituwu (ed.), *The Multi-Disciplinary Approach to African History*. Choba: University of Port Harcourt Press, 1997.

6. If this sounds a little too deterministic, let me say that I am suggesting some important necessary conditions, but *not* the sufficient conditions, of the direction taken by Alagoa's thought. As Professor Afigbo reminded us at our gathering, without the addition of a creative spark unique to Alagoa, nothing constructive or out of the ordinary might have come from this combination of circumstances.

7. Notably: *The Ijaw Nation in the New Millennium*. Port Harcourt: Onyoma Research Publications, 2004.

CHAPTER 9: THE X-FACTOR IN THE LIFE OF AND WORK OF PROFESSOR E.J. ALAGOA

1. From personal observation and association with Prof. E.J. Alagoa of over 30 years.
2. Conversations with various members of the family, most recent interviews with Lady Mercy Alagoa (JP) and David Alagoa.
3. "This I believe" article on personal philosophy by E.J. Alagoa: *The Philosophies and Personal Histories of 24 Nigerian Achievers*, 2004 by Dipo Ajayi.
4. *Beke You Mi, Nembe against the British Empire.* Onyoma Research Publications, 1995.
5. *The People of the Fish and Eagle: A History of Okpoama in the Eastern Niger Delta*, 1995.
6. *Uses of Hindsight as Foresight: Reflections on Nigerian and Niger Delta History*, 2004.
7. With Tekena Tamuno: *The Land and People of Rivers State.*
8. *The Land and People of Rivers State.*
9. *The Land and People of Delta State.*
10. *The Akassa Raid 1895.*
11. *The Small Brave City-State: A History of Nembe.*
12. *Jaja of Opobo: The Slave Who Became King.*
13. (with Fombo) *The Chronicle of Grand Bonny.*
14. *A History of the Niger Delta: An Historical Interpretation of Ijo Oral Tradition.*
15. *Okpu: Ancestral Houses in Nembe and European Antiquities on the Brass and Nun Rivers of the Niger Delta*. Onyoma Research Publications.
16. The Bibliography of Prof. E.J. Alagoa's work.
17. *Kali kulu kulu kalika: A Check-List of Kalabari Drum Lore.* G.O.M. Tasie - Supplement to *Journal of Niger Delta Studies*, 1999.

II. SELECT BIBLIOGRAPHY FROM THE CHAPTERS

Note: Numbers in square brackets after an entry in this Select Bibliography indicate the Chapter(s) in which the reference is cited.

Afigbo, A.E. (1980). "The Eastern Provinces under colonial rule", in Obaro Ikime (ed.) *Groundwork of Nigerian History.* Ibadan: Heinemann Educational Publishers. pp. 424-483. [SUPL4]

Afigbo, A.E. (1993). "Colonial historiography", in Toyin Falola (ed.) *African Historiography* London: Longman. [4]

Afigbo, A.E. (1997). *The poverty of African historiography.* Lagos. [6]

Afigbo, A.E. (1986). *K.O. Dike and the African historical Renaissance.* Owerri: Rada Publishing Company. [6]

Agiri, B.A. (1998). "The historian: Ebiegberi Joe Alagoa", in N.C. Ejituwu (ed.) *The Multi-Disciplinary Approach to African History: Essays in Honour of Ebiegberi Joe Alagoa.* Choba: University of Port Harcourt Press. [4]

Ajayi, J.F.A. (1980). "A critique of themes preferred by Nigerian historians", *Journal of the Historical Society of Nigeria.* Vol. 10, No. 3. [6]

Ajayi, J.F.A. (1985). "Keynote Address: Factors in the evolution of political culture in Nigeria". in J.F.A. Ajayi and Ikara Bashir (Editors). *Evolution of political culture in Nigeria.* Ibadan: Ibadan University Press. [SUPL4]

Ajayi, J.F.A and Ikara Bashir (Editors) (19 85). *Evolution of political culture in Nigeria.* Ibadan: Ibadan University Press. [SUPL4]

Ajayi, J.F.A. with E.J. Alagoa (1980). "The re-orientation of historical studies: Sub-Saharan Africa", in *International Handbook of Historical Studies: Contemporary Research and Theory.* Georg G. Iggers and Harold T. Parker (Editors). Westport: Greenwod Press. pp. 403-418. [6]

Ajayi, J.F.A. (1998). "Beyond continuity and change: The past and the future in African historiography", in N.C. Ejituwu (ed.) *The Multi-Disciplinary Approach to African History: Essays in Honour of Ebiegberi Joe Alagoa.* Choba: University of Port Harcourt Press. [4]

Alagoa, E.J. (1960). *The Akassa Raid, 1895.* Ibadan: Ibadan University Press. [4], [9]

Alagoa, E.J. (1964). *The Small Brave City-State: A history of Nembe (Brass) in the Niger Delta.* Wisconsin: University of Wisconsin Press; Ibadan: Ibadan University Press. [4], [9]

Alagoa, E.J. (1970). *Jaja of Opobo: The Slave Who Became King.* London: Longman. [9]

Alagoa, E.J. with A. Fombo (1972). *A Chronicle of Grand Bonny.* Ibadan: Ibadan University Press. [9]

Alagoa, E.J. (1972). *A history of the Niger Delta: An historical interpretation of Ijọ oral tradition.* Ibadan: Ibadan University Press. [3], [4], [6], [7], [9]

Alagoa, E.J. (1976). "Dating Ijọ oral tradition", *Oduma,* Vol. 3 No. 1, 19-22. [4]

Alagoa, E.J. (1978). "Oral tradition and history in Africa", *Kiabara: Journal of the Humanities* (University of Port Harcourt), Vol. 1 No. 1, 8-25. [4]

Alagoa, E.J. (1980). "The Eastern Niger Delta and the hinterland in the nineteenth century", in Obaro Ikime (ed.) *Groundwork of Nigerian History*. Ibadan: Heinemann Educational Publishers. pp. 56-72. [SUPL4]

Alagoa, E.J. (1980). "King Frederick William Koko of Nembe", in T.N. Tamuno and E.J. Alagoa (eds.) *Eminent Nigerians of Rivers State*. Ibadan: Heinemann Educational Publishers. [4]

Alagoa, E.J. (1981). "The Ethnographic dimension in oral tradition", *Kiabara: Journal of the Humanities* (University of Port Harcourt), Vol. 4 No. 2, 7-24. [4]

Alagoa, E.J. (1981). "Oral data as archives in Africa", *Kiabara: Journal of the Humanities* (University of Port Harcourt), Vol. 4 No. 2, 193-202. [4]

Alagoa, E.J. (1981). *The Python's Eye: The Past in the Living Present*. First University of Port Harcourt Inaugural Lecture, 1979. Choba: University of Port Harcourt Press. [4], [6]

Alagoa, E.J. (1981) (Editor). *The teaching of history in African universities*. Proceedings of a Conference at the University of Lagos in 1997. Accra: Association of African Universities. [6]

Alagoa, E.J. and Kay Williamson (eds.) (1981). *Ancestral Voices: Oral historical texts from Nembe, Niger Delta*. Jos: Department of History, University of Jos. (Jos Oral Literature and History Texts, Vol. 4). [4]

Alagoa, E.J. (1986). *Noin nengia, Bere nengia / More days, More wisdom: Nembe Proverbs*. Port Harcourt. [2], [6]

Alagoa, E.J. with **F.N. Anozie** and **N. Nzewunwa** (Editors) (1988). *The Early History of the Niger Delta*. Hamburg: Helmut Buske Verlag. [3]

Alagoa, E.J and **T.N. Tamuno** (Editors) (1989). *Land and People of Nigeria: Rivers State*. Port Harcourt: Riverside Communications. [9]

Alagoa, E.J. (1990) (Editor). *Oral tradition and oral history in Africa and the Diaspora: Theory and practice*. Proceedings of a Symposium. Lagos: Centre for Black and African Arts and Civilization. [6]

Alagoa, E.J. (1994). "An African philosophy of history in the oral tradition". in *Paths Towards the Past: Essays in Honour of Jan Vansina*. Robert W. Harms, Joseph C. Miller, David S. Newbury and Michelle D. Wagner, editors. Madison: African Studies Association Press. pp. 15-25. [2], [6]

Alagoa, E.J. (1995). *The People of the Fish and Eagle: A History of Okpoama in the Eastern Niger Delta*. Lagos and Port Harcourt: Isengi Communications. [9]

Alagoa, E.J. (1998). "An African philosophy of time". in Soulayman Bachir Diagne and Heinz Kimmerle (Editors). *Time and Development in the Thought of Sub-Saharan Africa*. Amsterdam and Atlanta. (Studies in Itercultural Philopsphy, Vol. 8) [2]

Alagoa, E.J. (Editor) (1999). *A history of the University of Port Harcourt*. Choba: University of Port Harcourt Press. [8]

Alagoa, E.J. (1999). *The Land and People of Bayelsa State: Central Niger Delta*. Port Harcourt: Onyoma Research Publications. [9]

Alagoa, E.J. (1999). *The Ijaw Nation in the New Millennium.* Port Harcourt: Onyoma Research Publications. [3], [7]

Alagoa, E.J. (2001). *Beke You Mi: Nembe against the British Empire.* Port Harcourt: Onyoma Research Publications. [4], [9]

Alagoa, E.J. (2001). *Okpu: Ancestral Houses in Nembe and European Antiquities on the Brass and Nun Rivers of the Niger Delta.* Port Harcourt: Onyoma Resarch Publications. [9]

Alagoa, E.J. (2001). "The dialogue between academic and community history in Nigeria". in Louise White, Stephan F. Miescher and David William Cohen (eds.). *African Words, African Voices: Critical Practices in Oral History.* Bloomington & Indianapolis: Indiana University Press. [5]

Alagoa, E.J. (2004) "Prof. E.J. Alagoa, Professor of History" in *This I Believe: The Philosophies and Personal Histories of 24 Eminent Nigerian Achievers,* Edited by Dipo Ajayi. Lagos: Prestige Associates, pp. 63-72. [2], [5] , [9], [10]

Alagoa, E.J. (2004) *The uses of hindsight as foresight: Reflections on Niger Delta and Nigerian history.* Port Harcourt: Onyoma Research Publications. [2], [3], [6], [7], [9]

Ayalogu, M.C. (1985). *Perceptions of the African Past: Ebiegberi Joe Alagoa and His Works.* Choba: University of Port Harcourt Library (Unipolib Bibliographic Series, No. 5) xiii, 45p. [9]

Ayandele, E.A. (1964). *Missionary impact on modern Nigeria.* London: Longman. [SUPL4]

Ayoade, J.A.A. (1984). "Time in Yoruba Thought", in Richard A. Wright (Ed.) *African Philosophy.* Lanham: University Press of America. [2]

Carr, E.H. (1961). *What is history?* London: Macmillan Press. [SUPL4]

Cookey, S.J.S. (1974). *Life and times of King Jaja of the Niger Delta (1821-1891).* New York: Nok Publishers. [SUPL4]

Dike, K.O. (1956). *Trade and politics in the Niger Delta.* Oxford: Clarendon Press. [4], [SUPL4]

Dike, K.O. et al. (1960). *Eminent Nigerians of the 19th Century.* Ibadan: Ibadan University Press.

Ejituwu, N.C. (1997) (Editor) *The multi-disciplinary approach to the study of African history: Essay in honour of Ebiegberi Joe Alagoa.* Choba: University of Port Harcourt Press. [6], [10]

Ejituwu, N.C. (2004). *Thesis, antithesis, synthesis: Niger Delta historiography in time perspective: An inaugural lecture.* Choba: University of Port Harcourt Press. [4]

Enemugwem, J.H. (2003). "The rhetoric of oral historiography," *Kiabara: Journal of Humanities* (University of Port Harcourt), Vol. 9 No. 1. [4]

Epelle, E.M. [1970?] *Opobo in a century.* Aba. [SUPL4]

Falola, T. (Editor) (1993). *African historiography: Essays in honour of Jacob Ade Ajayi.* Lagos: Longman Nigeria Plc. [6]

Fubara, D.M.J. (1983). "Physical conquest of the Niger Delta", Convocation Lecture, Rivers State University of Science and Technology, Port Harcourt. [SUPL5]

Fubara, D.M.J. (1991). "Use of integral space and geosciences technology for environmental hazard monitoring". Port Harcourt: IGST, RSUST. [SUPL5]

Fubara, D.M.J. (1992). "A call for world action to save the endangered environment of the Niger Delta", Memo of the Rivers Chiefs and Peoples Conference presented at the United Nations Conference on Environment and Development, Rio de Janeiro, Brazil. [SUPL5]

Fubara, D.M.J. (1993) "Application of space science and technology to coastal zone management". Port Harcourt: IGST, RSUST. [SUPL5]

Fubara, D.M.J. (1995). "Peculiar terrain and land mass factor issue in revenue allocation". Port Harcourt: IGST, RSUST. [SUPL5]

Fubara, D.M.J. (2001). "Redress of illusive peace and development in [the] Niger Delta". Contribution to Niger Delta Development Commission. [SUPL5]

Henige, D.P. (1974). *The Chronology of Oral Tradition.* Oxford: Clarendon Press. [3]

Hexter, J.H. (1961). *Reappraisal in history.* London: Macmillan Press. [SUPL4]

Horton, Robin (1997). "Some fresh thoughts on Eastern Ijọ origins, expansions and migrations", in N.C. Ejituwu (Editor) *The multi-disciplinary approach to the study of African history: Essay in honour of Ebiegberi Joe Alagoa.* Choba: University of Port Harcourt Press. [3], [10]

Jaja, S.O. (1991). *Opobo since 1890: A documentary record.* Ibadan: Ibadan Publishing Houses. [SUPL4]

Jones, G.I. (1963). *The trading states of the Oil Rivers.* London: Oxford University Press. [4]

Kariala Konsult (1999). "Hydrology and hydrodynamics of the Niger Delta". D.M.J. Fubara (Editor). Report for [the] Niger Delta Environmental Survey.

Mabogunje, A.L. (1988). "The debt to posterity: Reflections on a National Policy on Environmental Management", in P.O. Sada and F.O. Odemerho (Editors). *Environmental Issues and Management In Nigeria Development.* Ibadan: Evans Brothers. pp. 17-25. [SUPL4]

Mbiti, J.S. (1969). *African Religions and Philosophy.* London: Heinemann. [2]

McCall, D.F. (1964). *Africa in time perspective: A discussion of historical reconstruction from unwritten sources.* Boston: Boston University Press. [6]

Muroe, M. (1993). *Becoming a leader: Everyone can do it.* Lanhan: Pneuma Life Publishing. [10]

Nigerian Constitutional Conference (1958). Paper NC58. London. [SUPL5]

Obasanjo, O. (1999) "Nigeria will rise again", Post-Election Address. Abuja. [SUPL5]

Obasanjo, O. (1999) "National Reconstruction: My Vision, My Mission". Abuja. [SUPL5]

Okara, Gabriel (1958). "The Ijaw creation myth", *Black Orpheus,* No. 2, 9-17. [5]

Okoye, Mokwugo (1980). *Profiles in social adjustments: Embattled man.* Enugu: Fourth Dimension Publishers. [10]

Popoola, O. et al. (1999) "Report of the Presidential Committee on Development for the Niger Delta". Abuja: The Presidency". [SUPL5]

Rouse, A.L. (1946) *The use of history.* London: Macmillan Press. [SUPL4]

Ryan, R.K. (1960). *The Confessions of St. Augustine*. New York: Image Books. [2]

Tamuno, C.A. (2005). "Appointment as Emeritus Professor of History" (An unpublished correspondence, UPH/REG/SS.43/296 from Registrar, University of Port Harcourt to Professsor E.J. Alagoa, dated 12 July 2005). [10]

Tamuno, T.N and E.J. Alagoa (Editors.) *Eminent Nigerians of Rivers State.* Ibadan: Heinemann Educational Publishers. [SUPL4]

Tasie, G.O.M. (1999). *Kali kulu kulu kalika: A check-list of Kalabari drumlore.* (Supplement to *Journal of Niger Delta Studies).* [10]

Uya, O.E. (1973). *African history: Some problems in methodology and perspectives.* Ithaca, NY: Cornell University Press. [6]

Uya, O.E. and E.O. Erim (Editors) (1984). *Perspectives and methods of studying African history.* Enugu: Fourth Dimension Publishers. [6]

Vansina, Jan (1965). *Oral tradition: A study of historical methodology.* Chicago: Aldine Press. [3], [4]

Vansina, Jan (1973). *Oral tradition as history.* Madison: University of Wisconsin Press.

Vansina, Jan (1968). "The use of ethnographic data as sources for history", in T.O. Ranger (ed.) *Emerging Themes in African History.* London: Heinemann. [4]

INDEX

A

Abassah, P 3
Achebe, Chinua 111
Afigbo, A E iii, 1, 2, 59, 64, 127, 144
African history 65
African religions and philosophy 21
Ajayi, A 55, 106, 119, 143
Akassa Raid 72, 75
Akwa-Ibom State 159
Alagoa, Ebiegberi J iii, 1, 5, 144
Alagoa, Joe A 97
Alagoa, Maclean
Alagoa, Solomon Iruo
Alagoa, Mercy G 3, 106
Alaska 154
Aluminium Smelting Company of Nigeria (ASCON) 150
Andoni River 154
Anglican Diocese of Niger Delta 55
Anglican Mission 118
Antiquities Ordinance 76
Ardouin, C D 106

Arinze, E 106
Aristotle 5, 16
Armstrong, Bob 34
Associated Gas Re-Injection Act of 1979 156
Augustine of Targaste 16, 21
Awe, Bolanle iii, 1, 143
Ayoade, J A A 21

B

Basuo, Benjamin A 97
Bayelsa State 159
Bayelsa State Elders Consultative Council 54
Bell-Gam, Winston I iii, 3, 165
Berber philospher 16
Berkeley, G 23
Biriye, Harold Dappa 157
Bonny River 154
Boro, Adaka 15
Brown, B S iii, 171
Bupo, G O N 138

C

Canada 155
Carnegie Fellowship 32
City of God, The 17
Cronon, D 59
Curti, M 64
Curtin, P 59, 71

D

Delta State 159
Derefaka, A A iii, 2, 133
Dike, Kenneth Onwuka 32, 45, 46, 49, 71, 118, 119, 120, 145

E

Egein, E 108
Ejituwu, Nkparom C iii, 1, 107, 144
Ekine (Sekiapu) 74
Ekong, Donald E U 59, 85, 86
Ekwueme, Laz 84
Ellah, Francis J 86
Enemugwem, John H iii, 1

Erekosima, Tonye 139
Ethnographic data
   Definition of 47
   Use of 47
Ewoama 97, 117
Exclusive Economic Zone Act of 1978 156

F

Federal Environmental Protection Agency (FEPA) 156
Fiofori Tam iii, 137
Fubara, Dagogo M J iii, 149

G

Gabriel, Amakievi O I 107
God is Mother: A Historical Review of Women in the Development Niger Delta Communities 74
Government College, Umuahia 58, 78

H

Historical Society of Nigeria 123
History of the Niger Delta: An Historical Interpretation of Ijo Oral Traditions 46, 49, 72
Hope Waddell Training Institute 58
Horton, Robin iii, 2, 29, 121
Howat, G M D 106
Humanism 10

I

Idahami (time concept) 20
Igben, Mamerhi J. iv
Ijaw History Project 1, 124
Ijo 12, 46, 52
  Origins of 128
Ijọ Nation in the New Millennium 73
Ikara, Bashir 13, 106
Imo River (Opobo River) 153, 154
Institute of African Studies 33
Intangible Cultural Heritage Project 55

J

Jaja, Dandeson Douglas (King of Opobo) 3, 146
Jaja of Opobo: The Slave Who Became King 44
Jaja, S O Sunday iv, 138
Jaja Village 144
.Japan 155
Jones, Gwilym I 45, 46, 49, 120

K

Kalaibiama 151
Kalajoe, Joseph 97
Kalama 151
Kambasa (Queen of Bonny) 73, 74
Ke 83
King Boy Amain 106
King Jaja Foundation 135, 148
King Jaja of Opobo 73, 141
Knowledge 22, 23
Koko (Amanyanabo of Nembe) 73, 140
Kotangora, Mamman (General) 152

L

Land Use Decree of 1978 150, 156
Logan, Rayford 64

M

Mabogunje, Akinlawon L 144
Mahadi, Abdullahi 1, 2
Mangite, Tuamain 97, 100, 117
Mbiti, John 21
Miers, Suzane 59
Minima Agreement 146
Mkpong (time concept) 19
Mobil oil spill 153, 154, 155

N

Nana Olomu 141
National Antiquities Commission 122
National Archives 43
National Archives Committee 122
National Inland Waterways Authority Decree of 1993 156
National Museum 141
National Trust 141

Nduka, Otonti 76
Nembe 6, 97
Nembe Ibe Road Projects Group 54
Niger Delta 6, 12, 32, 33, 43, 44, 47, 157, 158, 159, 160
Niger Delta Development Board (NDDB) 158
Niger Delta Development Commission (NDDC) 151, 163
Niger Delta University 36
Nigerian Antiquities (Symposium) 75
Nigerian Association for Oral History and Traditions 76
Nigerian Civil War 75
Nigerian History School 40
Nypapalm vegetation 151
Nzewunwa, N 106

O

Oba Ovonramwen [of Benin] 140
Obanya, Pai 106
Obasanjo, Olusegun 161
Ockiya, Daniel Ogiriki 70, 118

Odili, Peter 169
Oduma 83
Ogbulu, Ebitimi Banigo 51
Oglafa, Perrin 3
Ogoloma 83
Oil Mineral Producing Areas Development Commission (OMPADEC) 151
Oil Pipelines and Lands Decree (1993) 156
Oil Terminal Dues Act 156
Okara, Gabriel 2
Okochiri 83
Okorobia, Atei M iv, 2, 111
Okpoama 51, 95, 117
Oloibiri 155
Ombu, Jigekuma A iv
Onyoma Research 53
Opobo 133, 145
    Historical Notes of 165, 171
    War Canoe House of 166
Opobo Constitution *see* Minima Agreement
Oral Tradition 43
Oral Tradition: A Study in Historical Methodology 45
Orji, Kingdom E iv, 111

P

Pearse, Sereba A-K iv, 2
People of the Fish and Eagle: A History of Okpoama in the Eastern Niger Delta 51
Petroleum Act (1990) 156
Petroleum Decree (1969) 156
Philosophy of History 7
Plato 16, 17
Python's Eye: The Past in the Living Present 100

Q

Qua Iboe River 153
Queen Kambasa of Bonny 73, 74
Queenstown 151

R

Resource Control 163
Reverend D O Ockiya College of Theology and Management Sciences 55

Rivers Research Scheme 121
Rivers State 159
Rivers State Readers Project 122

S

Saikiripogu 83
Saro-Wiwa, Ken 58
Sekiapu (Ekine) 74
Slave Routes Project 55
Small Brave City-State: A History of Nembe (Brass) in the Niger Delta 44, 77
Socratic aporetic method 5
South East Asia 155
Sultan of Sokoto 144

T

TSSK Theatre Company 3
Tantua, Diseye 3
Tagaste 16
Taylor, Alan J P 106
Time 16-22 *passim*
Trade and Politics in the Niger Delta [K O Dike] 45, 145
Trading States of the Oil Rivers [G.I. Jones] 45
Treaty of 1884 [Opobo] 141

U

Udoidem, S I iv, 1, 5
Unesco 55
United States of America 155
University College (Ibadan) 118
University of Wisconsin 119
Uses of Hindsight as Foresight 7-28 *passim*, 73, 192
Uya, Okon E iv, 1, 144

V

Vansina, Jan 32, 45, 48, 71, 118, 119
Vincent, Theo 85

W

Waritimi, Pius 2
Ways of the Rivers 139
Williamson, Kay 34, 76, 121
Willink's Commission 157, 158
World Bank 157

X

X-factor 91

www.ingramcontent.com/pod-product-compliance
Lightning Source LLC
Chambersburg PA
CBHW031551300426
44111CB00006BA/261